Community Research as Empowerment

Community Research as Empowerment

Feminist Links, Postmodern Interruptions

Janice L. Ristock and Joan Pennell

Oxford University Press
Toronto   New York   Oxford
1996

Oxford University Press
70 Wynford Drive, Don Mills, Ontario M3C 1J9

Oxford New York
Athens Auckland Bangkok Bombay
Calcutta Cape Town Dar es Salaam Delhi
Florence Hong Kong Istanbul Karachi
Kuala Lumpur Madras Madrid Melbourne
Mexico City Nairobi Paris Singapore
Taipei Tokyo Toronto

And associated companies in
Berlin Ibadan

Oxford is a trademark of Oxford University Press

Canadian Cataloguing in Publication Data

Ristock, Janice L. (Janice Lynn)
    Community research as empowerment: feminist links,
postmodern interuptions

Includes bibliographical references and index.

ISBN 0-19-541080-7
1. Community - research. 2. Community power.
3. Feminism. I. Pennell, Joan 1949- . II. Title.
HM131.R58 1996   307'.072 C96-931248-2

Design: Max Gabriel Izod

1 2 3 4 — 99 98 97 96

This book is printed on permanent (acid-free) paper ♾.

Printed in Canada

To our parents,

Bob and Jan Ristock
and
Kitty and Tom Stern,

and our partners,

Catherine Taylor
and
Charley Pennell,

who nurtured our commitment to empowerment

Contents

Preface

An Invitation

This volume is intended as an invitation to take part in reshaping the way community research is carried out, to make it consistent with aims of empowerment. We invite others to consider what empowerment research is, how it is done, whether they should use it, and, if so, when and where. In our discussions with community activists and government officials, as well as university students and faculty, we have found an interest in such research growing alongside uncertainties about its meaning, procedures, and validity. These mixed reactions make sense at a time when society remains dependent on technology but increasingly suspicious of the aims and results of science as conventionally practised. There is a desire for research dedicated to empowerment but also a fear that such research will be biased by its commitments to social change, and thus produce false and possibly harmful conclusions. Some respond to this indecision by treating it as one more symptom of a postmodern malaise in which we can trust nothing, including science, and urge a return to doing 'normal' research. We prefer to take it as a call for creating a 'postmodern' space—one that is open and unfixed—in which to test alternative research strategies.

We believe that our discussion of the methodology that we term 'research as empowerment' will be helpful in:

1. filling a gap in the existing literature by outlining empowerment research processes, from developing the research focus to releasing responsible analyses;

2. exploring the research process from a feminist community-building perspective that promotes co-operative efforts while affirming distinct cultures;

3. demonstrating ways of incorporating multiple methods within the framework of research as empowerment; and

4. bringing forward postmodern insights, which challenge all tightly held beliefs, including our own, without relinquishing the empowering ethos of affirmative approaches to research.

We have developed this research approach on the basis of our experiences in studying efforts to end violence against women and children and to create democratic organizations. Working in these areas has focused our attention on empowerment as a strategy both for contributing to social action and for conducting our research. It has also heightened our awareness of the importance of the two apparently contradictory elements that make up our subtitle. 'Feminist links'—between researchers and the communities we work with, between our research methodologies and our social-action agendas—follow from seeking a coherent feminist praxis through a network of interrelated commitments; 'post-modern interruptions' are the incongruities we encounter in the search for such a praxis—the contradictions, gaps, and complexities that a postmodern perspective reveals, which keep us from inappropriately fixing on any one analysis or solution. The examples in this book show that there is no single route to research as empowerment; in fact, the routes are multiple.

JANICE: My interest in writing this book stemmed from my awareness, as a community researcher and Women's Studies professor, of the lack of such a reference. In teaching a course on feminist approaches to research, it became clear that I had a particular perspective that informed my own research with community groups, and that this approach was worth writing about. I was committed to presenting an unsanitized view of the research process that would be useful for many constituents and that would bring forward some of the exciting implications for social research of feminist postmodernist approaches. I was familiar with Joan's insightful writings and the connection between her interests and mine in the areas of violence against women and children and building democratic relations. After a conference at which we were both panelists, I invited Joan to take part in writing this book with me.

JOAN: I accepted this invitation because I enjoyed discussing methodological issues with Janice, whom I had found to be flexible yet firm in her thinking. In the course of writing this book, I came to appreciate all the more her ability to foster 'feminist links and postmodern interruptions' that challenged my thinking. As a social-work educator, I found that this approach to research seemed to offer a way of carrying out research that was both practical and ethical. At another level, the project appealed to me because of my religious commitments as a member of the Society of Friends (Quakers) to attend to the wisdom within each person and to bring all these insights together towards the creation of a non-violent and caring society.

Our collaboration on this book involved many 'links and interruptions' as our ideas expanded, changed, and re-formed. Separated by great distances, communicating most often on e-mail, we read and commented on each other's work as respectful critics who helped to tease out one another's experiences and 'truths'. Perhaps, above all, our own collaborative process has been a matter of linking our many shared commitments—to feminism, to social justice, to respecting difference—across our differences in analytical tendencies and social locations, which we both came to respect.

We could not have written this book without the participation of many people along the way. The examples we cite came out of extensive work with others committed to research as empowerment in women's, First Nations', and young people's organizations. Some of these individuals played a direct part in preparing the examples in two of the chapters: Eveline Milliken, Maureen Flaherty, Mallory Neuman, and Shirley Flamand at the University of Manitoba; Sharon Perrault and Betsy Hudson at Ma Mawi Wi Chi Itata; Sharon Taylor, Cathy Forristall, Pat Power, Trudy Ryan, Janice Parsons, Gale Burford, Karen Ellison, Donna Hardy, Erin Keough, Fran McIninch, and Evariste Thériault on the Hoops and Hurdles Project; and Diane Molloy, Greg Warford, Michelle Sullivan, Jackie Gosse, Andy St John, and Gale Burford on the evaluation team of Choices for Youth. Among the other people involved in discussions of material in some chapters are Angie Balan, Rhonda Chorney, Gerry Pearson, Lynne Pinterics and Lee Woytkiw from the CLOSE project. Thanks also to Caroline Fusco, who assisted in preparing the bibliography and who has worked as a research assistant with Janice on many projects.

Our thinking has been repeatedly challenged and advanced through dialogue with community activists, students, colleagues, government bureaucrats, and funding representatives—diverse constituencies that in many cases also overlap and interact. Our thanks to the anonymous reviewer who provided helpful comments on the manuscript, as well as to the editors at Oxford, especially Euan White, whose support and encouragement we have appreciated from the beginning. The book has benefited from the fine editorial eye of Sally Livingston, who showed no patience for woolly language but much for us. Finally, we would particularly like to mention the contributions of our families: Janice's partner, Catherine Taylor, and Joan's sister, Yolanda Broad, who refined our understanding of cultural and discourse analysis (Catherine also provided invaluable editorial commentary on the entire manuscript); Joan's partner, Charley Pennell, who made sure that she had a space in which to write; our parents, Bob and Jan Ristock and Kitty and Tom Stern, and Joan and Charley's three sons, Ivan, Daniel, and Benjamin, who made clear the necessity of creating a future in which we all belong.

1

Empowerment as a Framework for Community Research

> I use empowerment to mean analyzing ideas about the causes of powerlessness, recognizing systemic oppressive forces, and acting both individually and collectively to change the conditions of our lives. . . . Empowerment is a process one undertakes for oneself; it is not something done 'to' or 'for' someone (Lather, 1991: 4).

Empowerment is a widely used, or perhaps misused, term that is increasingly invoked as a challenge to conventional approaches to community research. Its relation to such research is uneasy, however, because its application remains unclear. This uncertainty reflects widespread controversy over the meaning of empowerment and the absence of a developed framework for incorporating it in the research process. In this book, we reach into our experiences as participants in feminist and other emancipatory social movements to define empowerment and its relations to research methodology. Our connections with activists of differing views on power and empowerment have simultaneously affirmed our shared commitments and made it impossible to fix on any single position. These heterogeneous links and the interruptions they have prompted in our thinking have made it both possible and necessary for us to develop multiple and responsive strategies for empowerment and its embodiment as research.

Empowerment is a far-reaching term that is now being used in a wide range of professional and political contexts, academic disciplines, and activist movements. In general, to empower means to enhance our ability to control our own lives, or to 'develop a sense of collective influence over the social conditions of one's life' (Young, 1994: 48). On an individual level, this can mean drawing on inner strength to take control of a situation and assert one-self. Interpersonally, it can mean sharing resources for mutual benefit, or working together co-operatively. In professional relations, it often means facilitating and collaborating rather than prescribing and treating. Organizationally, empowerment can mean working democratically, partici-pating equally, and sharing in decision-making and policy development in the work environment. Finally, on a societal level, empowerment is a politi-cal activity that can range from individual acts of political resistance to mass political mobilization—usually of a relatively powerless group such as blacks, lesbians and gays, women, or aboriginal people—aimed at changing the nature and distribution of power in our society.

Empowerment as an approach to community research means thinking consciously about power relations, cultural context, and social action. It is an approach to building knowledge that seeks to change the conditions of peo-ple's lives, both individually and collectively. It involves consulting or collab-orating with diverse individuals, groups, and communities as part of the process of illuminating people's lives and social issues. Fundamentally, it is research that is 'committed to identifying, facilitating or creating contexts in which heretofore silent and isolated people, those who are "outsiders" in var-ious settings, organizations and communities, gain understanding, voice and influence over decisions that affect their lives' (Rappaport, 1990: 51).

We agree with Lather (1991) and Rappaport (1990), who stress the social-change agenda of a research process centred on empowerment. As activist researchers, we work with people in their communities in order to facilitate understanding and change. We use the phrase 'research as empow-erment' to convey the idea that research itself can be a lived process of empowerment when it encompasses both a critical analysis of power and a reconstructing of power so that the latter can be used in a responsible manner.

The empowerment framework for research that we are outlining brings together our commitment to feminism, our readings in the area of postmod-ernist thought, our disciplinary backgrounds in community psychology and social work, and, finally, our experiences as both researchers and practitioners, which have focused on violence against women and children and its converse, democratic social relations. As feminist activists, we have each endeavoured to direct both our research and our practice according to the visions and strategies of the women's movement.

However, our experiences have not been entirely parallel. Janice's work, primarily with feminist social-service organizations and lesbian communi-ties, has focused on developing training programs on heterosexism and homophobia and exploring organizational structures that are consistent with feminist principles. Joan's work with programs for women and young people, white and aboriginal, has involved building connections between different groups of women, across the women's and labour movements, and community, university, and government bodies. No doubt readers will hear our different social and professional lives in our voices. The diversity of our experiences has made us aware that there is no single approach to empowerment, and that many research methods can be used within this framework. The common thread has been our growing awareness of the necessity of attending to and reworking power differences within research relationships.

FEMINIST LINKS, POSTMODERN INTERRUPTIONS

In the history of the feminist movement, the primary means of empowerment has been women's telling of their own stories. From the early consciousness-raising groups of the late 1960s and early 1970s to the present, women have been encouraged to come forward and give voice to their realities as a way of beginning to change the oppressive and constraining conditions that still exist. Our guiding examples are the women who, in speaking out against the rape, incest, and abuse they have experienced, have provided the catalyst and the knowledge required to develop services and bring about changes in policies and laws. Feminists have developed service programs such as shelters for battered women and their children, women's resource centres, and sexual-assault agencies (Ristock, 1991b) and coalitions for these programs (Pennell, 1990c) that operate with an empowerment philosophy. Although constrained by funding requirements and professional and bureaucratic ideologies (Potucheck, 1986; Srinivasan and Davis, 1991; Walker, 1990), a number of these organizations have developed creative strategies to put in place collective or participatory structures (Pennell, 1990b; Ristock, 1993; Rodriguez, 1988). These instances of empowerment have fostered links between women in the common struggle to name and eradicate violence.

Nevertheless, some feminists have recently become critical of the ideology of empowerment. This criticism is in part a reaction to the way politicians, bureaucrats, and professionals have taken empowerment to mean nothing more than individual self-assertion, ignoring the societal factors—including fiscal policies, legal processes, and employment practices—that disadvantage women and children. However, the criticism also reflects a rethinking of the directions and strategies of the women's movement. In particular, feminists have learned that efforts to work towards solidarity and sharing power do not always take adequate account of the differences among women (Yuval-Davis, 1994). Challenges to this homogenizing view of empowerment have come primarily from women at the margins, for whom age, race, sexuality, disability, or some other aspect of their identity makes for an uneasy fit with a fixed category that specifies the 'essential' properties or characteristics of all women. Such essentialism reduces their experiences to irrelevant deviations from the 'norm'. Conceptualizing empowerment as including an analysis of power not only between men and women but also among women makes it possible to forge links across differences without obscuring those differences. This perspective moves us away from theories that universalize and generalize towards an analysis of the shifting power relations in any social context. Relations are not fixed as either 'power over' and 'power with'; rather, they form and re-form in various combinations.

The world today is in what has been described as a postmodern moment (Giroux, 1991) in which international corporations contend for global hegemony (through control of technology, information, and currency flows) and are resisted by democratic movements—feminist, labour, anti-colonialist—with their own competing interests. The Enlightenment faith in rationality and science as the means of determining universal truths and realizing human emancipation has been shattered by experience. What were once assumed to be natural laws applying to every time and place—such as the innate aggressiveness of all men and the innate passivity of all women—have been revealed not as the fruit of rational inquiry but as rationalizations for violence, hierarchy, and exploitation. Public confidence in scholarly objectivity has been weakened by growing awareness of the material interests and ideological prejudices that have a profound influence on the consciousness and practices of researchers, and hence on the conclusions drawn from their work.

Foundationalism—the faith that the rational scientist produces knowledge free from historical and current pressures—has been eroded by the postmodern recognition that knowledges are plural and are not 'discovered' but 'constructed'. The positivistic stance—that valid and useful knowledge is derived from logical deduction and empirical observation—has, unaccustomedly, to exert itself to maintain its hegemony (Dallmayr and McCarthy, 1977). What were once touted as universal truths are now characterized as 'grand narratives', or all-encompassing stories that exalt the views of particular communities (Lyotard, 1984). The resulting upheaval has led to the development of a postmodern epistemology, or theory of knowledge, that is conducive to research as empowerment. In particular, it challenges the desire to create universally authoritative statements—a desire that must be resisted if empowerment is to be a process that 'one undertakes', not something that is done to or for someone (Lather, 1991).

This volume uses the language of feminist postmodernism, one of three dominant feminist epistemologies identified by Sandra Harding (1986; 1987); the other two are feminist empiricism and feminist standpoint theory. While all three epistemologies claim that feminist science produces better knowledge than the traditional kind, they do so for different reasons. Feminist empiricism advocates the inclusion within scientific communities of feminist researchers on the grounds that they will produce more objective (positivistic) research, unskewed by androcentric bias. Feminist standpoint theorists agree that feminists do better research, but not because of their more faithful adherence to positivistic norms; rather, they claim that the struggle to achieve a feminist standpoint grounded in awareness of women's subordination makes for a more comprehensive and ethical understanding than is possible for their masculinist counterparts, even those who hold emancipatory goals. In turn, feminist postmodernists have criticized feminist standpoint theorists for seeming at times to assume that women's experiences can be reduced to a single standpoint; rather, they encourage the development of multiple awarenesses or discourses responsive to the diversity of women's experiences. Although they dispute one another's claims, each of these feminist epistemologies is above all concerned to counter the androcentrism of the intellectual tradition out of which it emerged, whether the invocation of objectivity to obscure masculine bias, the espousal of revolutionary agendas to mask an investment in male supremacy, or the splintering of women's lives into micro-narratives to consolidate misogynist discourses.

Depending on the context, each of these feminist epistemologies (along with others) can advance or hinder feminist aims, and we recognize their contributions to our past and current research. We have chosen to emphasize the postmodern perspective in this volume because it draws attention both to the larger cultural shifts that are occurring at community and global levels (postindustrialism, postcolonialism) and to the theoretical shifts that are taking place within academic arenas. Although some authors use 'postmodernism' and 'poststructuralism' interchangeably, while others distinguish between them (Burman and Parker, 1993), we have found that the former term incorporates all the levels at which our research is directed.

Postmodernism is not inconsistent with feminist analysis, but it takes us to a different level of inquiry. Where conventional feminism might lead us to examine the social conditions of women's lives, a postmodern feminism enables us to see the many ways in which discursive conditions affect women's lives. Gayatryi Spivak (1987: 249) has written of the influences of feminism and postmodernism as 'persistent interruptions of each other'. Our approach to research is to take up the interruptions that postmodernism brings forward while also building links through the use of empowering practices. We believe that this approach has important implications for research on violence against women and children.

Much of the feminist research literature on violence relies on either empiricist or standpoint approaches (Gorman, 1993; Stanley and Wise, 1993; Swigonski, 1993). Standpoint approaches, in particular, are consistent with an empowerment framework in their concerns for praxis (joining theory with practice), reflexivity (awareness of what one is doing and why), and critique (examining power relations within a gender analysis). The drawback to both empiricist and standpoint epistemologies is their common assumption that there is a single social world and physical reality for the scientist to discover or the political activist to uncover.

More specifically, feminist research on violence often brings forward women's voices and women's experiences of violence as a way to expose the roots of violence and lead to social action (Gelles and Loeske, 1993; Kelly, 1988). Gender and power are the main components of this analysis, which offers the all-explanatory story or 'grand narrative' that violence is used to maintain social control over women. In many cases this research has the emancipatory goal of eradicating violence against women, a goal we certainly support; yet some of our research experiences have caused us to question our own reliance on the grand-narrative analysis of violence assumed in most feminist research. For instance, Janice's work on violence in lesbian relationships points to the inadequacy of theories of violence that are based exclusively on heterosexual relationships and male perpetrators. Similarly, Joan's work with aboriginal communities and with young people suggests that the meaning of abuse is constructed and reconstructed—in other words, that it depends on which voices (male/female, adult/youth, etc.) within any cultural group are highlighted. Adhering too rigidly to theories that have been developed to explain violence can prevent us from thinking creatively about it.

These interruptions encountered in our work on violence against women and children have caused us to take a closer look at the analytical practices commonly used by postmodern researchers. In particular, we have considered deconstruction (taking apart social categories as a way of seeing how one's world is constructed) and discourse analysis (examining language and ideologies as a way of understanding how meanings are produced; Parker, 1992) and their implications for an empowerment framework. Discourse analysis allows us to look at how language operates to sustain oppressive practices. For example, Janice's work on lesbian abuse (see Chapter 4) follows the principles of discourse analysis in asking and analyzing interview questions—who is speaking? from what identity? from what gender and sexuality perspective? in what historical, societal, and cultural framework? from what relational perspective?—that make it possible to understand how lesbians make sense of their experiences of abuse. Their voices and their constructions of their experiences are placed at the centre of analysis (as described by Brown and Gilligan, 1992; Gavey, 1989; Parker, 1992). At the same time, their words are deconstructed to analyze the ways in which their experiences have been constructed through the interplay of various competing ideologies. By attending to the specific ways in which public discourse structures and limits our thought, making some thoughts unthinkable, researchers can begin to imagine how to disrupt the terms of dominant discourses so that other ideas, perhaps less oppressive in their social consequences, become thinkable. Experiences alone (as often employed in standpoint research) cannot explain the complex dynamics of abuse.

Discourse analysis and deconstruction are useful tools for developing new theoretical insights not only into the underlying causes of abuse but also into potential alternatives. A case in point is the experience that Joan gained through varied involvements with anti-violence programs in Canada and the US. As a founder of a shelter, she discovered that deconstructing its statement of philosophy helped her to stand back from the document, which she had helped to write, and to identify the conflicting ideologies that generated incompatible goals (Pennell, 1987). She was then able to reconstruct a more coherent set of guiding principles. As a consultant for another shelter, she was able to identify the competing orientations held by the board (business), staff (feminist), and volunteers (charity) in order to help sort out their differences on how the house should be operated. As a facilitator in groups for abused women, both white and aboriginal, she listened for the divergences in members' discourses in order to foster a discussion in which the women could draw on the strengths of their cultural heritages (see Chapter 2). Finally, in her research on the shelter movement, she studied how participants combined seemingly incompatible notions of organization to create innovative alternatives such as 'democratic hierarchy', in which ownership is centralized in a board of directors while decision-making is carried out by a range of stakeholders (Pennell, 1990b), and 'consensual bargaining', in which labour and management advance their separate interests while reaching agreements that compromise neither (Pennell, 1990a).

Yet additional questions are raised by the influences of feminism and postmodernism within our empowerment framework. How can we deconstruct our research findings and at the same time maintain with confidence our goal of clearly defined action? Who benefits from this way of doing research? What voices will be heard? How will work with communities be facilitated by this approach? These are questions that will be addressed throughout this text. Bringing feminism and postmodernism together in the context of empowerment means rejecting universalizing narratives while at the same time taking a firm political stance, affirming real people and their needs for social justice while at the same time destabilizing or *disrupting* categories that are socially constructed in order to reveal the workings of power and make it possible to imagine alternative ways of thinking that will generate less oppressive relations.

Teresa de Lauretis (1987) captures our position in her writings about the category 'woman'. She describes how, on the one hand, as feminists we want to hold on to the category of woman because of its significance in our social reality, while on the other hand we recognize that this category (which includes very disparate types of people) must be subject to ongoing reconstruction in our efforts for social change. In the same way we want to hold on to our recognition of the materiality of violence and its effects while recognizing that we construct violence through the processes of social inquiry. For example, in Janice's work on lesbian abuse (Ristock 1991a; 1994; forthcoming), 'battering' is a thoroughly constructed notion, a form that falls outside the dominant definitions of battering. The fact that the concept 'battering' is constructed does not in any way lessen the impact of being battered. Yet deconstructing the concept 'battering' is actively empowering because, in disrupting existing constructions, we begin to move past their dangerous social effects (for example, the tendency of lesbians not to seek help for abuse in their relationships because of the heterosexism in the currently dominant constructions of battering; see Ristock, 1994).

The same principles apply to the term 'empowerment'. The current understanding of this term is derived in large part from work with individual women, such as assertiveness training, releasing anger, improving interpersonal skills, and raising self-esteem. An unreflective transfer of this individualistic view of empowerment to work with men can serve to aggrandize men further at the expense of women and to divert attention away from systemic inequities (see Dankwort, 1988, on the psychologizing of male battering); similarly, introducing this concept in the context of work with young people can be inappropriate if it means ignoring their developmental needs for guidance on how to relate in a non-abusive manner. In a study of a community-living program for youths (Burford, Pennell, and Burnham, 1992), Joan had to reconsider the meaning of empowerment in the context of a program with a predominantly young male clientele and an adult female staff: specifically, it was crucial for the program evaluators to identify the potential, in this situation, for too readily excusing youth for their actions and holding caregivers responsible. A belief in the feasibility of empowerment must be bolstered and at the same time this concept itself must be taken apart so that it can be redesigned in a manner responsive to the particular nexus of relationships.

If our work, whether with individuals, organizations, or communities, is to be truly empowering, we must be conscious of these dynamics of affirmation and disruption. Shane Phelan (1993: 786) refers to this double perspective as 'strategic essentialism':

> we have to stand where we are, acknowledging the links and contradictions between ourselves and other citizens of the world, resisting the temptations to cloak crucial differences with the cloak of universality and to deny generalities for fear of essentialism. Only in this way will we be free from the domination that lives both within and around us.

We have to resist binary ('*either/or*') constructions of social reality and challenge ourselves with constructions that can include '*both/and*' or '*neither/nor*'. For example, we need both to hold abusers accountable for *their* actions and to hold all of *us* accountable for recreating a society in which we are neither abused nor abusing. The intention of our research is to create 'links and interruptions' with others in a process that can lead to understanding and liberation.

RESEARCH AS EMPOWERMENT

> **Research as empowerment:** an approach to research that seeks to effect empowerment at all stages of the research process through critical analysis of power and responsible use of power.

Our definition of research as empowerment has gone through many reworkings and will probably go through more. The definition in the box encloses and fixes its meaning for us at this particular time and gives us a framework within which to test, contest, and reconfigure. Reflecting on our divergent and complex experiences of studying violence and democratic relations has pushed us to reconsider our own tightly held principles of feminist research. Our thinking has been loosened through an ongoing process of looking at what we have done, contrasting our respective strategies, and checking them against other feminist methodologies. This process has led us to see any research methodology as a culture, a set of norms or sanctioned practices for carrying out research. It has also led us to identify 'links and interruptions' as essential features of a research method centred on empowerment. The 'links' open our research to a wider group (which may include researchers, participants, and the people who will use the research findings or be affected by them) and keep our studies grounded in diverse realities; the 'interruptions' prevent our thinking from becoming either rigid (by excluding too much) or amorphous (by including too much).

Central to this culture is the assumption that good research (that is, valid and ethically supportable research) requires that researchers critically analyze their own power and use it responsibly. To analyze power critically means to bring both material and discursive perspectives to questions of power: How do differences in the material conditions of researchers and research participants complicate the empowerment process? What patterns of language serve to perpetuate oppressive power relations? How might our own language-use lock us into unempowering relations with the communities we work in as researchers/collaborators? What assumptions about the causes and effects of violence, the perpetrators and victims of it, can be seen in the way we talk about and research violence? Following Foucault in his attention to the processes and 'strategies' of power, in our own critical analyses of power we ask 'Who exercises power?' and 'How does it work?', as well as 'How does it happen?' (Kritzman, 1988: 103). Our view of power, then, is that it is relational; it is not a fixed entity that can be surgically removed, given away, or done without. Of course we do want to work against oppressive power relations, both in society and in our own research relationships; but that is not to say that power is always negative or repressive. To use power responsibly as researchers means to strengthen, not diminish, our capacity to affect the world while holding ourselves accountable for our actions. Rejecting, neutralizing, or even reversing power distributions between researchers and research participants is not our aim. Although we believe that modern society suffers from an imbalance of power along lines of gender and other constructed criteria, our experiences have shown that research as empowerment may shift, analyze, and even change power differences, but it does not remove them.

This discovery ran counter to our original premise that research as empowerment must entail either eliminating power or redistributing it equally among researchers and research participants. That premise seemed consistent with our feminist politics and professional practice, both of which emphasized collaborative efforts; we recognized the need to minimize power inequities in all relationships, including the research one, through critical reflection and openness to criticism from others. Further reflection, however, complicated our notion of empowerment: in practice, acting responsibly may sometimes mean keeping or taking on power in order to put in place measures to constrain abusers of power. The researcher who uses her academic credibility to lobby for shelter funding is making appropriate use of a form of power not shared by the research participants. It is not enough to attend to the distribution of power within activist/research efforts; we must also attend to the impact of our efforts on the distribution of power in the larger social world. We are left, then, with this reformulation of the problem of power: not 'How can we get rid of it?' but 'Within a particular context, do our efforts contribute to a critical analysis of power and responsible use of it?'

A culture of empowerment disentangles and reworks relations of power by making their previously obscured workings visible and therefore more open to disruption. In this section, we specify some of the principal methods for critical analysis and responsible use of power in community research. As the following chapters will show, these practices have been central features in the methodology of 'links and interruptions' that we have developed in our studies on violence and democratic relations.

'Alternative Truths'

A culture of 'links and interruptions' shifts power so that alternative truths can be constructed through reflection on people's diverse experiences. To realize this aim, research as empowerment employs strategies that overlap with those used in participatory action research. Participatory action research seeks to create usable knowledge by involving the researched as researchers in social analysis and action (Stull and Schensul, 1987; Whyte, 1991). Rooted in the pragmatic philosophy of the American educator John Dewey, this approach combines reflection and action to generate 'learning by doing', and knowledge is assumed to be established when people reach consensus that it has disposed of a problem (Friedmann, 1987). While Dewey evaded the question of whose experience forms the basis of this consensus, standpoint theorists in the field of participatory action research have asserted that, in the case of oppressed peoples, such research establishes a new relationship to knowledge in which marginalized people are encouraged to develop their views and are affirmed as authoritative sources of knowledge (Alary, Guédon, Larivière, and Mazer, 1990; Maguire, 1987). We agree with their position but would add Yuval-Davis's (1994: 193) caution that alliances across groups of oppressed peoples can lead to 'self de-centring, i.e., losing one's own rooting and set of values' if the values and beliefs of individual participants are incompatible with one another. We would also add that these incompatibilities can disappear as different discourses permeate one another and push towards new formulations.

Shared interests are not the beginning point of consensus but rather its conclusion (Barber, 1984); and these conclusions are never final. Agreements can always be reworked as people reflect on their impacts in changing contexts. Research as empowerment fosters consensus among diverse people precisely because it affirms their connections while disrupting their assumptions. To engage in this process, researcher and participants alike need to work actively to create a milieu in which they can attend to each other's experiences, views, differences, and uncertainties, and at the same time build a sense of mutual trust that will allow them to move forward together. Thus Janice, in Chapter 3, discusses a consultative process in which organizations can work to build democratic relations and begin to see how organizational cultures are constructed; and Joan, in Chapter 6, describes how creating a set of 'images' of unionized shelters made it possible to move beyond divisions based on mutually exclusive positions. Out of such processes comes the possibility of forming new understandings about people and issues, creatively combining differing perspectives, and reviewing and re-forming earlier interpretations. The goal is not to uncover some static truth; the truths propounded in words are discursive, socially constructed, and consensual, not fundamental or proven through research. Nonetheless, they can be a legitimate basis for action towards reducing human suffering and increasing freedom.

'Inclusive Communities'

Research as empowerment constructs alternative truths as a way of speaking out against inequities; but in so doing, it faces what Linda Alcoff (1991) refers to as 'the problem of speaking for others'. Research as empowerment does not eliminate this problem. However, the practice of creating 'inclusive communities' helps us to deal with it in a socially responsible manner. Research as empowerment seeks to include within its research communities individuals and groups who are likely to hold alternative views. Thus it involves people in research who are not conventionally thought of as having the knowledge and skills to design, conduct, or appraise research. These individuals may take part in the research in a variety of capacities: as researchers (see Chapter 2, on Joan's collaborative research with aboriginal women and students), consultants (see Chapter 3, on Janice's work as an organizational consultant), research participants (see Chapter 4, on Janice's data collection with feminist collectives, shelters, and lesbians who experienced abuse in their relationships), or research evaluators and users (see Chapter 6, on Joan's analysis of shelter unionization). Whatever role these people assume, research as empowerment seeks to shift power relations so that their views are taken into account.

One way or another, most of the chapters in this volume continue the theme of 'inclusive communities'. Chapter 2 presents accounts by two research groups, in which Joan participated, of their strategies for forming inclusive working relations: respectively, 'bridging the gaps' and 'having a balance'. In Chapter 3, Janice interrupts unified notions of 'inclusive communities' by describing the insider–outsider position of an organizational consultant. In Chapters 4 and 5, Janice describes the processes involved in research design where using multiple methods and being aware of power relations and our locations in the research contribute to bringing forward diverse perspectives that are part of 'inclusive communities'. And in Chapter 6 Joan points out that even when the researcher is analyzing the data on her own, the use of mutually contradictory methods fosters 'inclusive communities' by keeping the analysis open, respectful, fluid, and inventive.

Transparency and Reflexivity

Research communities, even those with participants from many walks of life, run the danger of closing themselves off from other ways of seeing the world. Opinions can congeal into fixed positions unless the study is laid open to inspection. Standard research norms promote such openness to the extent that investigators are expected to specify the means they used to answer their study's question and to disclose any data that pertain to their conclusions. In research as empowerment, however, the methodological area that must be open to scrutiny is enlarged to include the power relations operating in the research process.

To this end, feminists and others have called for transparency (Klein, 1986; Stanley, 1993) and reflexivity on the part of the researcher (Fonow and Cook, 1991; Gouldner, 1971; Stanley, 1990). 'Transparency' means revealing who one is and how one's location shapes the research process (Klein, 1986); 'reflexivity' means including oneself in what is being studied (Hammersley and Atkinson, 1983). Together, these would appear to make it possible for researchers to assess their own as well as others' contributions to the power dynamics. In our experience, the difficulty is that the 'who' does not remain constant: it fluctuates, splits, and re-forms depending on personal history and context. Without the individual autonomy presupposed in the modernist thinking that postmodernism undermines, the sense of self or subjectivity can no longer be seen as a fully unified and rational consciousness (Giroux, 1991).

Although this instability leaves us susceptible to having our identities defined for us, it also makes it possible for us to collaboratively redefine our identities. In research as empowerment, people form 'inclusive communities' in which they can construct alternative grounds of relation. For example, in Chapter 2 Joan describes the formation of inclusive research groups in which the members, having together discerned oppressive identities, were able together to construct new ones more congruent with their beliefs. And in Chapter 5 Janice describes the intricate power plays that have an impact on how individuals present their identities and that can make the ethical principles of reflexivity and transparency difficult to put into practice.

OVERVIEW

The following chapters use examples from our own research experience to illustrate our efforts to put into a practice a research framework of 'links and interruptions', the quandaries we have faced, and the successes we have achieved. Readers will note that we have written most of the chapters separately, highlighting our individual experiences. Although we have critically reflected and commented on each other's work, we have by no means attempted to submerge the differences between us, since we see those differences as consistent with our open, unfixed research framework.

This volume is not a how-to book in the tradition of research-methods texts intended as introductions to the subject; rather, it is an exploration of a particular research orientation. Although the presentation of certain issues broadly reflects three basic stages of the empowerment research process—from developing a research focus (Chapters 2 and 3) to research design and process (Chapters 4 and 5) to creative analysis of data (Chapter 6)—the focus is not on steps and techniques. Rather, we conceptualize the many aspects of the research process as a series of concentric circles or layers that resonate out from one another: circles rather than steps because we do not leave one set of concerns behind as we move on to another, but instead shift our emphasis as the work proceeds, while continuing to keep all aspects of the research process in sight. Our chapters reflect this conceptualization of the research process: The inner circle, or core, of our approach is the goal of engaging in research for social change—this is what gives our projects focus. The next circle reflects our empowerment approach to research, which means critically analyzing and responsibly using power. The third circle consists of process issues such as reflexivity, transparency, bridging gaps, having a balance, flexibility, and power plays. A fourth circle consists of what are commonly referred to as research steps: defining a focus, building researchers' relationships, securing funding, designing the study, collecting data, producing creative analyses, disseminating the findings, and acting on the results. The fifth circle is our concern for research outcomes such as alternative truths, renewal and development, 'inclusive communities', and accountability. Finally, the outermost circle is our framework of feminist links and postmodern interruptions.

Chapter 2, 'Building "Inclusive Communities"', focuses on the creation of 'inclusive communities' across racial lines. The first account depicts the formation of a research collective of students and faculty to compare student experiences of feminist education in primarily white, main-campus settings, and an inner-city class consisting of aboriginal people and recent immigrants. The second describes the working relationships developed by Joan and two aboriginal colleagues involved with a group for aboriginal women dealing with family violence. In Chapter 3, 'Researching Organizations for Renewal and Change', Janice challenges the conventional view of research as taking place outside the day-to-day processes of groups, organizations, and communities, and shows how consulting can serve as a kind of collaborative inquiry, fostering growth and renewal, through a case study concerning the introduction of workplace democracy in a women's mental health clinic. In Chapter 4, 'Multiple Methods for Validity', Janice specifies how to select and utilize diverse modes of data collection for studying others and self in the context of community. The chapter explores ways of building multiple methods into the research design and, equally important, maintaining the flexibility required to expand and revise the design once research is in progress. A study of feminist social-service collectives and a training and education project for workers in shelters and second-stage housing illustrate how diverse methods (interviews, surveys, analysis of internal documents, focus groups, and researcher reflexivity) can be combined to achieve greater insight. In Chapter 5, 'Power Plays', Janice identifies the power struggles that occur within research relationships and presents strategies with broad implications for acknowledging and playing out power relations. In particular, she describes her own experiences in researching, first, feminist collectives and, later, abuse in lesbian relationships. Discussing the struggles of lesbians doing lesbian research and the issues of safety, ethics, and identity politics that emerged in her work, she concludes with guidelines for lesbians doing lesbian research. In Chapter 6, 'Creative Analyses', Joan examines the problem of generating creative analyses in an ethical manner, outlining four principles that she used to diffuse binary thinking and promote dialogue and co-operative action among workers and management at a number of unionized shelters for abused women. Finally, in Chapter 7, 'Unity, Disruption, Transformation', Janice and Joan together summarize some of the main themes and recommendations of the preceding chapters and reflect on future directions for research as empowerment in an era marked by both anti-feminist backlash rhetoric and neo-conservative economic policies. To illustrate the need for research that considers the effect of discursive conditions on material ones, Janice discusses the example of a needs assessment regarding lesbian abuse. In the second part of the chapter, Joan offers two examples of how research and evaluation can be used to persuade funding bodies to continue their support for worthwhile projects. The first example outlines the community-building research process followed by a team of anti-poverty activist and academics, while the second describes the evaluation of a community-living program for young people that was created in response to the closing of Mount Cashel Orphanage after allegations of child abuse.

Recognizing that the language used in this book may not be familiar to some readers, we have appended a glossary of frequently used terms. In addition, the appendices provide examples of research instruments, including consent forms, questionnaires, and interview frameworks, that may assist others in designing their own studies.

2

Building 'Inclusive Communities'

> I had gotten to the point of being paralyzed by waiting and wanting to do participatory research perfectly (Maguire, 1987: 157)

If, as Patti Lather (1991: 4) claims, empowerment is not done 'to' or 'for' someone, how can researchers initiate empowerment studies on anyone other than themselves? Would it not be contradictory for them to impose a research question and design? And wouldn't these contradictions be all the greater when the research in question concerns people of a different race from the researchers? But if no one launches the study, how does it get under way? This was the dilemma that Patricia Maguire (1987) faced when she arrived at a New Mexico town adjoining the Navajo Nation and the Pueblo of Zuni.

As a doctoral student, Maguire wanted to do participatory research with women, native and non-native, who had been battered by their partners. However, for nearly a year she was unable to see how she could begin her work when the abused women were not asking her to participate in research with them. In fact, she was spending the time quite productively, working at the local shelter and making connections with women who might eventually take part in the research. Through these experiences, together with reflection on the actual practice of participatory research, she came to realize that adherence to the ideal of total deference to the wishes of the participants was setting impossible constraints on any action she might take. She became mobilized by forming 'feminist links' with the women involved and by 'interrupting' the intimidating discourse of some theorists of participatory research.

In our view, research as empowerment forestalls paralysis for three main reasons. First, it cannot demand conformity to certain processes because empowerment does not follow a pre-set route. In particular, research as empowerment, while often carried out in collaborative working groups, does not require such a format. It may well involve researchers and participants with different degrees of involvement in the process. In this respect it diverges from participatory research (e.g., Stull and Schensul, 1987; Whyte, 1991), with which it otherwise holds much in common. (In Chapter 3, for example, Janice discusses research as empowerment in the context of her experience as an external consultant working with established organizations.)

Second, even though it does not require a formal participatory group, research as empowerment does not leave the researcher floundering alone to determine the research question and design. The research question comes out of social action to reshape power relations; and the reflexivity that is an essential part of research as empowerment (see Chapter 4) ensures that researchers continuously check their questions and answers with those affected by the research.

Third, research as empowerment strengthens its practitioners. While countering oppression entails risk, empowerment promotes the building of confidence, skills, and support networks. As participants, both the researcher and the researched, reflect on what they are doing, they learn about themselves and their own uses and misuses of power, and reaffirm their belief in the possibility of change. Research as empowerment may appear daunting, but we know from experience that it can produce hope, vitality, and solidarity.

This chapter presents the feminist strategies developed by two groups to build 'inclusive communities' across racial lines. Both projects took place in Winnipeg, Manitoba, a city in western Canada with a rich history of radical action and a strong presence of First Nations peoples. The first group consisted of feminist students and instructors in a university social-work program; the second was formed by the facilitators of a support group for aboriginal women who had been abused by their partners. As a member of both of these groups, Joan worked with the other participants—aboriginal and white—to compose accounts explaining how we structured our ways of working together.

Research as empowerment encourages moving into and out of various communities, as opposed to restricting participants to one allegiance. Women of colour have repeatedly pointed out that forcing people into a single identity—whether it is based on gender, race, class, or sexuality—advances colonization, isolation, and violence (hooks, 1990; Lorde, 1984; Mies, Bennholdt-Thomsen, and Werlhof, 1988); and First Nations women have noted the irony that their identity as women has been used to erase their entitlements to their native land (Bear with Tobique Women's Group, 1991). In the two examples presented here, the participants maintained and developed numerous affiliations in addition to their shared roles as researchers, and in this way fostered 'inclusive communities'. The effort to create 'inclusive communities' provided each group with the attachments, tension, and vision to focus their work and to consolidate their identity as a group. Because the concept of 'inclusive communities' provides the framework for pulling together the accounts of the two groups, I will begin by discussing it.

First, however, a cautionary note: although the use of group examples in this chapter has the advantage of giving collective renditions of the experiences, it may leave the false impression that research as empowerment can take place only in a group context. Chapters 5 and 6 discuss doing this type of work individually.

'Inclusive Communities'

> **Building 'inclusive communities':** bringing together people from diverse backgrounds and social positions while at the same time constructing a firm identity as participants in a process based on respecting separate identities.

Throughout this volume, the term 'inclusive communities' is enclosed in quotation marks as a reminder that it is a concept that should be approached with caution. Not only have our experiences with creating 'inclusive communities' been rife with contradictions, but the phrase itself is an oxymoron, since the word 'community' implies exclusion: every community is distinguished from all others by boundaries that establish where it begins and other ones end. As Iris Marion Young (1990: 300) points out, the 'ideal of community' is 'politically problematic . . . because those motivated by it will tend to suppress differences among themselves or implicitly to exclude from their political groups persons with whom they do not identify'. Rather, she advocates a 'politics of difference . . . giving political representation to group interests and celebrating the distinctive cultures and characteristics of different groups' (1990: 319).

While Young is astute on the failings of the dream of community, her proposed solution falls short. Linkages may already exist within and across divergent groups; progressive change can involve first disentangling and then rejoining these ties. The goal is not to discard communal connections but to make room for the differences that separate us. In the groups under examination in this chapter, the integrity of the collectivity was reinforced by interspacing inclusions and exclusions among the members and between the group and outside forces. As abused women know too well, affiliations both bond and bind. To keep 'inclusive communities' from becoming another form of entrapment, we had to loosen and even cut some ties (particularly with abusers), fasten some (especially with other people seeking control over their lives), and reattach others (with family and friends from whom the women had become estranged). In reknotting our ties, we constructed alternative senses of our identities. Although the wording may sound awkward, 'inclusive communities' are referred to in the plural to emphasize the multiplicity and variability of identities.

Rendering Accounts

> **Accounts:** a means of holding ourselves accountable both to others and to ourselves for our critical analysis and responsible use of power.

Each of the two research groups prepared an 'account' reflecting on its experiences and sharing them with others. Rendering these accounts was a way of holding ourselves responsible both to others and to ourselves. By reflecting on our work and its power dynamics, we were able to judge the experience according to the criteria of empowerment: were we critically analyzing and responsibly using power?

The term 'accounts' serves as a reminder that these presentations are our particular construction or retelling of our past experiences and are influenced by our social contexts, individual psychologies, and group interactions (see Kitzinger, 1987). The modesty of the term prevents us from swelling our renditions of the research process to 'metanarratives' applicable to all times and places—'grand truths' that would serve to control other people's thinking and keep them from being responsible for rendering their own accounts. At the same time, 'account' is substantial enough to prevent reducing these narrations to what the postmodernist Lyotard (1984) calls 'little stories'; such story-telling would tend to fictionalize the presentations and absolve their authors from speaking with honesty and depth.

By agreeing to take part in the accounting process, the participants re-affirmed the significance of our work together and the significance of our connections with each other. As one participant later remarked, the group 'was more important looking back than I realized at the time'. She further observed that the 'process is on a continuum—things are not over—we are still processing now what happened. We needed the distance to articulate it better.'

Each group agreed that I would pull together our recollections and that all participants would check the account before its publication. As far as possible, I have sought to retain the language of the participants. Each example begins with an overview of the project in question and then presents, in the words of the group members, the key strategy that was developed in each case for working together in a manner that created 'inclusive communities'.

The following examples illustrate the close relationship between research as empowerment and involvement in movements to effect social change. Instead of starting with pre-set questions, these research efforts were motivated by a sense of the urgency of finding solutions to social injustices. The specific research questions that were developed reflected the philosophical frameworks of the movements from which the participants drew inspiration—in particular, the movements for the emancipation of women and First Nations—including those movements' analyses of gender, race, and class. In each case, the participants' efforts to transform society became identifiable as research when we were able to delineate a specific issue about which we wanted to learn and to which we wished to respond with a critical analysis and responsible use of power: this became our research question.

Framing the research question: the focus of the study

· emerges from participation in efforts to change society;

· reflects the philosophies of the social movement inspiring this social action; and

· becomes a research question when it is consciously articulated.

In preparing each account, I have identified one main strategy developed by the group to overcome barriers to forming 'inclusive communities', and, from a synthesis of the participants' comments, pointed out the strategy's strengths and limitations. The first example highlights the limitations of the attempt to create 'inclusive communities' within a research collective composed of white women. The second example, in which the primary focus was not research at all but facilitating a group for abused aboriginal women, suggests ways of resolving the problems posed by the first example, but this strategy too has limitations. The experiences described here may assist other groups wishing to create 'inclusive communities', but before the strategies suggested can be useful they must be adapted to suit the particular situation.

1. ASSESSING FEMINIST EDUCATION

The first group was a research collective made up of students and faculty from the University of Manitoba's main-campus school of social work and its branch inner-city program at the Winnipeg Education Centre. The main-campus program had a predominantly white Canadian enrolment, while the inner-city program admitted students who were aboriginal, recent immigrants, sole-support mothers, and welfare recipients. We formed this group in 1989, shortly after the Faculty of Social Work had proposed terminating courses that focused on women's and First Nations' issues. The proposal to eliminate these courses brought protests from students and instructors, and the Faculty eventually voted to retain them.

Nevertheless, we remained gravely concerned about the courses' long-term survival. For this reason, although we had no funding support, we resolved to document the impact of the women's-issues courses on both the main and inner-city campuses and how this impact was achieved. Thus we had two research questions: What were the effects of feminist social-work education on students from different cultures? And by what means were these effects realized? We limited our study to the women's-issues courses even though as individuals we had spoken out in favour of the aboriginal-issues courses as well, on the grounds that a group of white feminists should not take charge of research regarding the aboriginal courses.

By including representatives from both the main-campus and inner-city programs, we situated ourselves to examine feminist education through the lenses of gender, class, and culture. From students' responses to a question-naire, as well as interviews, we learned that feminist education made a lot of sense to mainstream and non-mainstream students alike (Pennell et al., 1993). However, we also learned that marginalized students in main-campus classrooms retained a minority status that inhibited their full participation, while in the inner-city program they could freely claim feminism as their own.

Bridging the Gaps
Feminist social-work education research group[1]

> I was feeling mighty 'pissed off', cynical, tired, hopeless and powerless. At times in the faculty I was clearly seeing the way it was and felt no change was possible. I was to the point of not caring—let me do my work and get out the door (Research group member, 1993).

We entered the group from different positions within the Faculty of Social Work. To pull our individual experiences together, we have employed a metaphor developed by three of the group's participants. Eveline, Mallory, and Maureen spoke of the research group as 'bridging the gaps' generated by the university. As they explained, 'by bringing together tenure-track, con-tingent, sessional instructors with master's students, [and] bachelor students, there was a joining together that overcame those artificial (but heavily adhered to) boundaries.'

'**Bridging the gaps**': building partnerships across social differences.

Joining ranks

Before joining the research group, many of us were already acquainted as practitioners, activists, and friends; and as women and mothers we shared a sense of the importance of feminism in our lives and for our children. Within the university, we had also had the opportunity to size each other up in advance. As an undergraduate student, Naomi knew Joan as an instructor; and the two graduate students, Mallory and Maureen, had been in Joan's courses. In addition, Maureen had been a teaching assistant for Joan, and Mallory had been hired as a sessional instructor for one of the women's courses. Thus both Maureen and Mallory entered the group with the dual perspective of student and instructor. Eveline, with a contingent appointment at the inner-city program, came to the main campus for various committee meetings, in the course of which she had the opportunity to observe Joan, who had the more secure tenure-track, main-campus appointment. From working together, all of us had come to respect each other's insights and skills and to trust that we would relate with openness and honesty, despite the power differentials between us. Eveline explained that we were able to 'leap' the 'gaps' because the 'commonality of feminism was greater than the boundaries' fencing off students and faculty from each other; and as feminists we were 'comfortable in using first names from the start' and 'set up a respecting group where Joan didn't establish what it was going to be. Instead we really talked with each other. Mallory, Maureen, and Eveline saw this experience as raising a bridge between them and research itself. As one of them explained, 'doing the research made things I was doing more "valid"; [it gave me] more confidence to talk with others about [the study] and other research. Working together demystified "research". It took the fear out of it. Research is now interesting. Knowing that research could be accessible, practical, applicable, relevant to women's experiences. . . . Women can do research in a way that is important. I read feminist research books and say "I've done that!"' Seeing themselves as qualified researchers, they were able to enter into the study group as real partners.

Respecting separations

Eveline was the group's connection to Shirley, an aboriginal student at the Winnipeg Education Centre. Shirley was comfortable relating to the research group through Eveline, with whom she had worked extensively. She agreed to collect information from her classmates but declined our invitation to join the group. Although we would have preferred that Shirley become a full member, we respected her decision and appreciated the contribution that she chose to make.

Shirley's decision made sense in that we were white women all situated, with the exception of Eveline, on the main campus. In Eveline's words, the women who decided to join had 'already tested out' the others in a way that was not possible for Shirley. The separation of Shirley and the research group, however, went beyond interpersonal relations. It was also a function of structural barriers between the main and inner-city campuses, ones that Eveline's rank and skin colour helped her to surmount only in part.

Based at the inner-city campus, Eveline and Shirley were well acquainted with the racism and classism that threatened the existence of their program. Faculty and students there were proud to be participating in a program that not only offered a solid education in social work but was accessible to disadvantaged students: the very people who would have the richest insights into the situations of many of the profession's clientele. However, the Centre was constantly required to justify its budget because its students received greater cost-of-living and tuition support than did students on the main campus. With the future of the program still in question, the status of both faculty and students was precarious. The instructors lacked job security, and the students were uncertain whether they would have a program to complete and, if they graduated, whether they would be accepted by employers as fully qualified Bachelors of Social Work.

But the gaps remained

Within our group, we fostered 'inclusive communities' and thereby gained a sense of achievement and support—a worthy accomplishment in a university context that bred cynicism and exhaustion. Yet in not attracting inner-city students to our group, we failed to close the gap between the main and inner-city campuses. As individuals we advocated continuation of the aboriginal-issues courses, but we restricted our research study to the women's-issues courses, feeling that it would be inappropriate for us, as white women, to take responsibility for research on the aboriginal courses. Contrary to all our intentions, though, our stance meant that in 'joining ranks', we never removed the ranks. Instead we closed out the more marginalized and maintained the academic structures, assigning the inner-city program a lower priority than the main-campus one.

Having reinforced this gap while rejecting it, we sought to bridge it by 'respecting separations'. When Shirley declined our invitation to join, we accepted her decision but were pleased that Eveline, teaching at the Winnipeg Education Centre, was able to negotiate with Shirley a way for her to contribute apart from the main-campus group. As long as the group remained located at the main campus, we continued to bridge the gaps without narrowing them.

2. Co-Facilitating an Aboriginal Group for Abused Women

This second account describes the process of building 'inclusive communities' in a context where Joan, as a white university professor, was very much an outsider. It was written in collaboration with Sharon and Betsy, two aboriginal women employed by an Anishinabe (First Nations) service agency in Winnipeg named Ma Mawi Wi Chi Itata, which had adapted the model of self-government to fit within an urban context (see Armitage, 1993). A significant part of this agency's mandate to help First Nations people to reclaim control over their lives and resources, and to re-establish communal caring, was to address the problem of family violence within the urban native community.

Sharon and Betsy co-facilitated support groups for aboriginal women who had been abused by their partners, and their work was being evaluated as one part of a larger study on how to design an anti-violence program within aboriginal traditions. Joan was invited to participate on a voluntary basis and to give Sharon and Betsy instruction on how to facilitate the group. The introduction of a white woman into an aboriginal group raised the question of what a non-native worker's role ought to be in a social agency expressly devoted to affirming its members' aboriginal heritage. We hoped to answer this question through observing and reflecting on our own participation in this process. Over the 16 weeks of the group we kept journals, we talked together as co-facilitators about the impact of Joan's presence, and in the end, after much reflection, we concluded that a white participant could make a worthwhile contribution, as long as the program stayed in the hands of the aboriginal community. Our experience is necessarily specific, but it illustrates how people can strive to find a balance that will allow them to work together across their differences.

Having a Balance

Sharon Perrault, Betsy Hudson, and Joan Pennell

Sharon and Betsy first met Joan outside the university clinic where the support group was to be held. All of us had arrived wondering whether it would be possible to include a third co-facilitator who was not only unfamiliar to the others but a white academic. After co-facilitating similar groups for three years, Betsy and Sharon had developed a rhythm for working together. Meeting them, Joan felt that they were trustworthy people with whom she could work. But Betsy and Sharon were more cautious; they wanted to see how Joan would relate with them and with the group members. Knowing that Joan was a professor, they expected her to take charge.

From the start we had to address the question of what it meant to introduce a white woman into an aboriginal program. We did not begin with this

> **'Having a balance'**: according greater weight to the more marginalized members of the group by giving them greater representation in numbers and, more important, by keeping within the language of their culture.

as a pre-set research question, and we had no formalized procedures for answering it. Rather, issues around Joan's presence repeatedly gained saliency over the course of the group sessions and compelled us to look for answers. In the tradition of participatory research, we learned by reflecting on our work together; and in the spirit of research as empowerment, we judged our work according to the standard of empowerment. In this context empowerment meant, in Sharon's words, 'having a balance' so that we could be partners in a society that tipped the power towards Joan. The meaning of Sharon's words—and the process we worked through to become 'inclusive communities'—can be understood within the framework of the Medicine Wheel, the spiritual guide for our work together. It served as an ideal against which to appraise our efforts to advance the group members' control over their lives and, more broadly, the goal of self-government for aboriginal peoples.

This account outlines the ways in which we learned to correct the imbalance of power by following the four sacred directions of the Medicine Wheel (or Sacred Circle), variants of which are found among many aboriginal peoples around the globe. Each direction on the circumference of the circle is viewed as offering a particular teaching, which must be combined with those from the other directions if the individual is to be in harmony with the universe (Storm, 1972). The aim is for people to visualize themselves at the centre of the wheel, rather than to fix their identity in any particular direction (Lane, 1984).

Turning clockwise around the Medicine Wheel, on the right side is the East, where we begin anew and receive the illumination to see far and wide; at the bottom is the South, where we develop the innocence and trust to touch our own hearts; on the left is the West, where we turn our thoughts inward to define our sense of personhood and power; and at the top is the North, where we find the wisdom to dwell in the Centre and take the path of least resistance, of detachment from worldly struggles, and of balance (Ma Mawi Wi Chi Itata, 1993; Storm, 1972). Each of the four directions is associated with a colour and represents one of the races of humanity (Lane, 1984), each of which is allotted an equal position within the universe.

The Medicine Wheel is a heuristic device for perceiving how all parts of the universe are interconnected and for achieving a balance among the parts through learning to *'Give-Away'* rather than hoard (Storm, 1972: 5). 'Giving away' is an act of healing and celebration for the giver, who neither expects reciprocation for the gifts nor passes judgement on the merit of their recipients. It is incumbent on practitioners of the Medicine Wheel to give service to others (Dufrene, 1990) and to respect the sanctity of all life forms, which are gifts from the Creator, and thus are to be shared equally by all living beings (Debo, 1970; Little Bear, 1986; Lyons, 1984). From the perspective of the Medicine Wheel, people are stewards or caretakers: they are helpers, not owners.

In this philosophy, healing is defined as re-establishing the balance among the various aspects of self—physical, emotional, cognitive, and spiritual. No one can tell another how to achieve such a balance. Thus the responsibility of the helpers is to 'give away' their knowledge, not to exercise it even on behalf of others. Unlike European-based approaches to healing, this approach is based on non-interference: sharing knowledge without diagnosing or offering prescriptions for cures.

In the language of the Medicine Wheel, the three co-facilitators, along with the women in the group, had embarked on a journey of healing. Our status as facilitators did not set us apart; while we had not experienced physical violence from a partner, we were all familiar with feelings of violation, and like the other women in the group we arrived with our energy drained, seeking affirmation, security, and renewal. By looking back at (re-searching) our experiences of violation we came to a better understanding both of those experiences and of the means of overcoming them in a sexist and racist society.

This account, structured according to the four directions of the Medicine Wheel, is based on Joan's journal notes (everyone composed her own notes privately at the end of each group session); her panel presentation, which was checked for accuracy by Betsy and Sharon (Pennell, 1991); materials from a manual that Sharon and Betsy helped to prepare on aboriginal family violence programming (Ma Mawi Wi Chi Itata, 1993); and lengthy subsequent discussions between Sharon and Joan. Each of these rethinkings turned us once again through the Medicine Wheel as we sought a balanced perspective on ourselves and the group.

The East: Beginning anew

When Sharon and Betsy first learned that Joan had been asked by an aboriginal colleague to co-facilitate a women's group with them, the plan seemed to add another stress to an already demanding job. They did not know Joan or how she would relate with the women in the group or with themselves. Moreover, for the first time the group was to be held not at Ma Mawi's premises but at the university's inner-city clinic. Although the new site appeared cold and inhospitable to Sharon and Betsy, they were prepared to explore both their new surroundings and their co-facilitator and to see if a working partnership could be established.

For her part, Joan had initially balked at the idea of joining the group. As an experienced group worker, she was willing to volunteer her time. But she was quite aware of her ignorance of Anishinabe cultures and worried that she would appear as an intrusive stranger. When aboriginal and white friends encouraged her to take part, eventually she agreed to participate on two conditions: that Betsy and Sharon consent to the arrangement after meeting with her, and that her role be redefined from 'training' to 'cultural exchange'. At the time, Joan did not know exactly what she meant by the latter term: only that it offered a vision of where to head. Over the course of the group sessions, its meaning gradually became clearer.

Each group session opened with a smudge ceremony in which those who elected to participate were cleansed by the smoke from a mixture of four sacred medicines—sweetgrass, tobacco, cedar, and sage (see Benton-Benai, 1988). As the gentle smoke wafted through the clinic, it helped to make the building into a place where the aboriginal women could feel at home. At the first session an elder joined us (as she would at each of the subsequent sessions when we were about to leave one direction of the Medicine Wheel and enter a new phase) to talk about the Medicine Wheel. She led the group by giving an account of her own life, and then, in turn, each of the members and facilitators gave an account of her life, with as much or as little detail as she chose. This sharing of our experiences as women in Canadian society helped us to draw closer to each other and enabled us to set forth together on the road to healing.

In the second session, Joan learned a better term to express what she had meant by 'cultural exchange' when a young woman who had kept very distant from Joan offered to read a poem that she had found helpful in reviewing her own life. Entitled 'Two Paths', it pointed to people's ability to choose their own life direction. At the end of the session, each of us wrote privately in our journals about what 'Two Paths' meant to us. Joan wrote, 'I have two paths. . . . My path is alone and not alone. For now my path goes amidst the Sweet Grass.' She was beginning to recognize that as a white woman in an aboriginal group, she had her own separate path; yet she could also accompany the other women on their path.

In the fourth session, the elder rejoined the group and helped to clarify the meaning of 'Two Paths' when she inquired about Joan's own religious beliefs as a Quaker. After listening to Joan's description, she pointed out parallels between the Ojibway and Quaker practices and gave Joan a sense of kinship with the Ojibway while affirming her own separate identity as a Quaker. Joan was learning that building 'inclusive communities' did not mean minimizing cultural differences, but rather maximizing understanding of herself and other people.

The South: Trusting

As facilitators, we knew that the group could not make this journey of heal-ing unless the participants could develop trust in each other, founded on a sense of safety and equality. The women in the group had been badly hurt both by their partners and by a society that lacked respect for their cultural heritage and concern for their economic and social disadvantages. Naturally uncertain about joining a group to discuss such a painful area of their lives, the women were already cautious about becoming close to others. Like most abused women, to protect themselves they had learned to watch closely those in positions of power. As facilitators, we were aware that the women took their clues on the workings of this group, in part, from studying how the three of us related with each other. In watching us, they were attempting to gauge whether this group would replicate their past experiences of domina-tion, especially given the facilitators' own differences in power.

Sharon and Betsy pointed out that the three facilitators formed a hierarchy in race and class. Betsy was a status Indian with legal entitlement to live on a reserve and receive benefits from the federal department of Indian Affairs, Joan was clearly identified as white, and Sharon, a Métis (French and Indian), was situated in the middle. In the context of the university clinic, Sharon and Betsy explained, these differences in skin colour ranked Joan at the top (a status reinforced by her socio-economic position as a university professor) and Betsy at the bottom. In the context of the Anishinabe social agency, however, the hierarchy was reversed, and full Indian status was accorded the highest rank. Likewise, the group members formed their own hierarchies of race and class, which in turn affected their relations with the three facilitators.

While the group members were scrutinizing the three of us as facilitators, we were monitoring our own interactions. As Sharon observed, Joan was being cautious about sharing in a strange milieu: she worried that she was 'off colour', both in her skin and in her behaviour. For their part, Sharon and Betsy were asking, 'Are we being graded? Are we being watched?' Without professional degrees, Betsy and Sharon assumed that their self-assessments would be given less weight than the judgements of Joan, the professor. Like her, they were figuring out what our contract of 'cultural exchange' meant and how it could be translated into actual practice.

Sharon pointed out that, despite all the barriers, we developed a rela-tionship in large measure because the three of us consciously set about form-ing a safety net. We met before each session, during the break, and afterwards in order to check out with each other what we saw happening in the group and how we should respond. In analyzing and planning sessions co-opera-tively, we formed and maintained connections not only cognitively but also emotionally and spiritually. We strengthened these connections by seeking out and giving feedback in private so that none of us lost face. Our comfort in working together grew as we learned more about each other in these separate sessions as well as through participation in group activities with the abused women.

Sharon and Betsy gradually came to trust Joan as they found that she laughed and cried with them, kept their private conversations in confidence, and did not try to take control of either the group sessions or the facilitators' separate discussions. Her body language alone indicated to Sharon and Betsy that Joan was not seeking to exert power over them. Without being particularly aware that she was doing so, Joan served as the link between the group and the university clinic and transformed an alien environment into a safe place for the participants.

Contrary to their expectations, Sharon and Betsy found that Joan was open to their religious beliefs and eager to learn. Their sense of spiritual identification with her grew on learning that, as a Quaker, she knew something about holding spiritual beliefs that put her in a minority. For her part, Joan was largely unaware of her effect on Sharon and Betsy, apart from recognizing that the three felt comfortable together. As a white woman, Joan took it for granted that she belonged at the clinic, and did not realize the extent to which Betsy and Sharon as well as the group members counted on her to speak up for their interests at the clinic and make it a safe place for them to meet in. Instead, Joan was keenly aware of how much she depended on her two colleagues to guide and protect her in an unfamiliar group. At the time, Sharon and Betsy did not realize the extent to which Joan relied on them, since they assumed that her status in itself would provide a solid sense of security. On later reflection, Sharon noted that she and Betsy, through their example as hosts, served as models for the manner in which the group members would respond to Joan as a guest in their midst. During the group sessions, though, we knew that we could count on each other because, as Betsy put it, 'We hit it off as people'.

Our ability to collaborate was based on a sense of both safety and equality. Sharon and Betsy pointed out a number of factors that served to equalize the power between them and Joan. First, we were all experienced in leading women's groups, and thus, in Betsy's words, started our work together 'coming from the same level'. Second, the fact that Sharon and Betsy outnumbered Joan helped to correct the imbalance between community and academe. And, third, Joan assumed what Sharon called a 'secondary role'.

As Sharon explained, Joan refrained from adopting the role of the expert and instead took her cues on how to behave from the aboriginal women themselves; in Sharon's blunt language, she 'sat on it'. Following the unspoken rules of another culture, Joan sensed the occasions, especially during discussions of aboriginal practices, when her presence was intrusive. At these times she slipped out of the role of facilitator or even participant into that of silent spectator. Joan knew better than to interfere, but she also felt that she could 'give away' control because Betsy and Sharon could be counted on to intervene in the group when necessary.

At other times, Sharon felt that Joan could have shared more of her knowledge and analyses and thus helped the group members to make more sense of their experiences of violence. Sharon and Betsy appreciated it when Joan took the initiative in introducing ideas and group work practices. They found that they could learn from her because she used what Sharon called 'the language of the group'. Joan respected aboriginal culture as she made the shift between her path as a white woman and her path as a companion to the group participants.

The West: Looking inward

Understanding within the group came not just through relating with others but also through looking inward as the women came to grips with the effects of violation on their minds and spirits. Rituals such as the smudging at the beginning of each session cleansed and prepared us for listening to our own feelings and thoughts, and writing our journals gave us a quiet time to reflect at the end of the meeting. In addition, three-quarters of the way through the sessions the group took part in a sweatlodge, a traditional ceremony of purification (Benton-Benai, 1988) that can become part of 'a Vision Quest to discover ourselves, to learn how we perceive of ourselves, and to find our relationship with the world around us' (Storm, 1972: 5).

For the sweatlodge, we travelled to the elder's reserve. Following various teachings and preparations we entered a tent and sat in a circle around a pit with hot rocks. Sitting for hours close together in the dark and heat was a profound experience, not to be spoken of with those outside the circle. Emerging late at night to a starry sky, we travelled back to Winnipeg, and on the way the young woman who had shared the reading of 'Two Paths' reached out to Joan for the first time and shared painful events in her life. She also offered to bring Joan a book on aboriginal ceremonies, a promise that she later fulfilled. After taking part in the sweatlodge together, this young woman and Joan reversed the standard roles with the young woman becoming the teacher on Joan's second path. Despite all the societal barriers separating the two, the experience they had been through together made it possible for them to connect on a spiritual level.

The North: Dwelling in the centre

The group concluded with ceremonies of celebration, and the three facilitators had their own ceremonies of closure. Until now, Sharon and Betsy had met with Joan either in the agency building or at the inner-city university clinic, but they decided to visit Joan in her familiar locales—her university office and home—to say good-bye before we took our separate paths. Finding her house warm and welcoming, like their own homes, they felt closer to Joan. For her part, Joan felt honoured by their visits and appreciative of their gifts of sweetgrass and sage. Since then our paths have recrossed at various points. A year later we took part together in a panel on aboriginal family violence programming and discussed how we had formed positive working relationships across our racial and cultural differences and built 'inclusive communities'. Joan continued to consult with Sharon, who always responded in a balanced manner by offering not only information and advice but also emotional support and spiritual guidance.

From their relationship with Joan, Sharon and Betsy took away another understanding of the academic world. No longer intimidated by a university professor, they could see that academics have their own limitations and that people outside the university have just as much to offer in the area of research. Sharon pointed out that meaningful research on family violence has to make sense to the people who are being studied. In order for such work to take place, people inside and outside the university must work side by side and 'give away' their skills and knowledge. Through such partnerships, research can be opened to the broader community, and studies can be oriented to take into account the various cultures of the research participants. In this way, the research becomes balanced.

But the balance is precarious

Both the aboriginal women's group and the subgroup of co-facilitators developed numerous strategies to create a balance; yet this equilibrium could be upset at any time. We needed an alternative world vision to rectify the unequal power accorded to Joan by society at large. Guided by the Medicine Wheel, we reweighted our own interactions so that Joan could accompany the aboriginal women on their journey of healing and find healing herself. The teachings of the Medicine Wheel would have been lost to us if the group had not been part of an aboriginal program whose adherence to its philosophy was sufficiently strong to withstand relocation to the university clinic. The ceremonies ensured not only that the group members followed their traditional ways but that Joan and the clinic itself were permeated by another world view. In affirming their own heritage, the aboriginal women were able to 'give away' to people of another race instead of keeping their ways to themselves. However, this exchange had to take place on the aboriginal women's terms: they had to determine the recipients, the pace, and the activities.

Building 'inclusive communities' meant that Joan had to respect the aboriginal group's decisions on when she should take part and when she should not. Despite the best intentions, attitudes alone would not have been enough to ensure this respect. The Anishinabe people had to have formal control of their own agency, including its funding, to fix in place their control over the group. Although the sessions were not held on its premises, the agency had the power, if it chose, to return the group to its home base and to remove Joan as facilitator (especially since, as a volunteer, she would not have had to be fired). The agency's control was reinforced by the discourse of the growing movement for First Nations' self-government, a language with which Joan was already familiar through her involvement in the women's movement. In the context of the women's group, exertion of control did not become a struggle with winners and losers. The Medicine Wheel guided all of us to 'give away' and, in so doing, to find a balance.

CONCLUSIONS

This chapter began with a question: Can we initiate research as empowerment that concerns anyone other than ourselves? Uncertain about the answer, Patricia Maguire felt paralyzed, unable to proceed with her doctoral research with abused women; she did not want to become one more researcher imposing a research agenda on aboriginal people. The two accounts presented in this chapter suggest that the answer lies in reframing the question. Research as empowerment does not isolate people by identifying some as 'us' and some as 'them'; it interrupts such binary thinking by simultaneously connecting and distinguishing individuals. The solutions described in this chapter, while not perfect, overcame to some extent the problems that arise in research across racial lines.

'Bridging the gaps' made it possible for the feminist social-work collective to 'join ranks' while at the same time 'respecting separations' between mainstream and non-mainstream Canadians. The limitation of this strategy was that the one aboriginal participant, although contributing to the study, remained outside the group, while the study itself remained focused exclusively on the value of the women's courses, and did not address the aboriginal courses. Going beyond 'bridging the gaps' to attempting to close them, the co-facilitators of the aboriginal women's group developed ways of 'having a balance' so that Joan could participate without tipping the scales towards her. Following the Medicine Wheel, a white woman could 'give away' power and accompany aboriginal women around the four directions. For their part, the aboriginal women were able to 'give away'—to share—their cultural practices without Joan's taking charge. Nevertheless, this balance constantly needed restabilizing in a racist society that throws all of us off centre and into unequal and unjust relationships. Clearly, the Medicine Wheel model that informed our efforts to work together in an empowering research process is not a feature of either postmodernism or feminism. However, it is a postmodern gesture to be open to whatever means of achieving our strategic goals are appropriate to the particular individuals involved. In this case, the powerful harmonizing principles of the Medicine Wheel provided a culturally intelligible framework for building 'inclusive communities'. Of course, not all research communities will have such models available. The important thing is to identify common ground among diverse people.

Despite their limitations, the strategies of 'bridging the gaps' and 'having a balance' offered healing from violation, cynicism, and exhaustion, and validation for research as an enterprise undertaken by a wide range of participants, not just men or white people or academics. In both groups, we needed an alternative discourse—whether feminist or Anishinabe—to give us guidance and strength in building 'inclusive communities' to which we could all feel we belonged. These strategies emerged out of our particular sets of relations and are not universally applicable. Our accounts are not intended as specific prescriptions but rather as a general examples of how the positive elements of different people's experiences, cultures, and discourses can be combined in creative and productive ways.

Note

[1] Shirley Flamand and Eveline Milliken at the University of Manitoba's Winnipeg Education Centre and Maureen Flaherty and Mallory Neuman at its main campus took part in preparing this account.

3

Researching Organizations for Renewal and Change

> Some researchers position themselves self-consciously, as participatory activists. Their work seeks to unearth, disrupt and transform existing institutional arrangements (Fine, 1992: 211).

In the last chapter, Joan discussed collaborative action projects that begin by building 'inclusive communities'. Here I will discuss another, very different way in which researchers committed to building democratic communities can work with established organizations on shared projects, but without constructing a shared identity.

Many organizations hire researchers as consultants to provide specific services such as conducting program evaluations, facilitating organizational development, and proposing interventions for organizational change. Most often this is time-limited contract work for which the researcher is paid either by the agency itself or by its government funder. In the course of such a project much research is done and much knowledge is produced, but because its objectives are action-oriented and internal to the organization, in many cases the work is not considered research and is not written up. Much of the literature that does describe such consulting work is written from a positivist, utilitarian perspective where critical analysis is minimal. Yet the opportunities for contributing to our knowledge of organizational dynamics and possibilities are considerable if the consultant has research in mind. Moreover, because consultants are typically called in at a time when the organization is open to structural change (often because it is addressing a crisis that calls for action), an empowerment framework may be particularly suitable for addressing issues of power and powerlessness and building new models and processes for enhancing participation. This chapter will focus on consulting as a way of intervening to bring about organizational renewal and development.

Both Joan and I have been particularly committed to working with social-service organizations that are developing participatory work practices. Our research-as-empowerment framework, with its emphasis on links and interruptions, reflexivity and transparency, provides a direction for short-term consulting work that can help both organizations and researchers to understand organizational culture and build empowering work environments. My own consulting work has most often been with feminist social-service organizations around issues of organizational development and organizational change. Typically small in size and economically marginal, these 'alternative' organizations tend to have a strong commitment to a shared purpose, to rely on volunteers (often recipients of the service) as well as paid staff, and to see their service work as involving them in the broad movement for social change (Richan, 1992; Ristock, 1993). Thus these agencies have been concerned with creating new social arrangements that minimize or eliminate dominant–subordinate relationships; this concern has also been central within their own organizational arrangements.

In my own research on feminist social-service collectives (see Chapters 4 and 5), one of the primary reasons that these agencies gave for operating as collectives was that they saw this as the structure most consistent with their analysis of violence against women as rooted in hierarchical social arrangements (Ristock, 1991b). In fact, many feminist service agencies want to realize values such as empowerment and equality in their operations. My work with such organizations has been to help them develop participatory democracies or collective structures, and use consensus decision-making processes more effectively. Although the paid consultant does not become part of an inclusive community, such consulting nevertheless presents opportunities to help make their operating environments more empowering both for the workers and for the women who use their services. In this chapter, the focus is on seeing practices for which organizations routinely hire consultants (assessments, trainings, program evaluations) as opportunities for doing research as empowerment to build workplace democracy.

Michelle Fine (1992: 229) has written about such opportunities in her work as a consultant to the Philadelphia Schools Collaborative, a large project aimed at restructuring the comprehensive high schools in that city: 'While tensions at the hyphen of consultant-activist-researcher are numerous, the gains of being in the change—for knowing, "eavesdropping", gathering varied points of view, and being able to orchestrate conversations around multiple stances—are enormous.' Although consulting is a practical, goal-oriented process, it can have a reciprocal relationship with theory. As consultants working in the area of feminist social services, we should be familiar with the extensive literature documenting such work and sharing strategies (e.g., Mansbridge, 1983; Morgen, 1983; Riger, 1994; Rothschild and Witt, 1986); and, in turn, we can contribute to this literature by documenting our own consulting processes and interventions, as well as the general understanding of alternative organizations. That said, there are important respects in which consulting differs from research. For instance, much as she values the rich vantage point of consulting work, Fine (1992: 229) points out that 'To take a static picture of [a site] at one point in time and call it research would be absurd' and to 'assume that I know all that must be told, or that all I know must all be told, would simply be naive'. Nevertheless, it is valuable to see such work as research and to write it down. Broadening the content of research as empowerment to include the situated findings of consulting work allows us another way of becoming participants in collaborative action. The goal of such research is not to make broad generalizations about feminist social-service organizations, but to develop critically reflective case studies of the negotiations involved in creating different social arrangements. We can use this work to examine moments that 'unearth, disrupt and transform existing institutional arrangements', as the quotation at the beginning of this chapter suggests. These examinations in turn can become part of a larger process of social inquiry.

When such work leads to publication, though, there are some methodological issues that demand consideration. If a consultant intends to produce a report for publication, provisions for informed consent, anonymity, and confidentiality should be clearly written into the consulting contract, in keeping with research ethics guidelines. In cases where a consultant who has not made such arrangements later decides to report on the process after all, anonymity can be achieved by excluding any identifying information from the published report. Informed consent cannot, however—by definition—be obtained after the fact. Researchers can still write about the process as long as we are reporting on our own experiences and observations and ensure that no harm results from the publication: by not identifying individuals or organizations, taking care not to quote any material that might identify the source, and reporting only on the areas that the organization agreed to include in the consulting process. Before releasing any report for publication, it is also good practice to have it reviewed by members of the organization, and by other researchers, if there is any question whatever about the adequacy of confidentiality provisions. In fact, any consultant who sometimes writes about projects should routinely seek informed consent. Especially important in the context of research as empowerment, such consent is part of the contract between researcher and participants that clearly lays out the assumptions, goals, and purpose of the research, the risks involved, participants' rights to confidentiality and anonymity, and the researchers' rights to document their own experiences within the project.

(See Appendix IV for the consent form used in a project described in Chapter 7.)

As Fine has written of similar dilemmas faced by counsellors collecting research information, 'the more explicit we can be with clients about the potential research purposes, and the more we can involve clients in writing about this material (e.g., to make "public" what are experienced as "private" and "personal" problems) the less damage we will do to the trust levels between ourselves and our clients/informants' (1992: 75).

INSIDER–OUTSIDER ISSUES IN CONSULTING

Organizational consulting is most immediately a collaborative problem-solving process (Richan, 1992). But the consulting process itself reflects certain political allegiances and locations for the consultant. The position of the consultant in relation to the organization, in turn, affects the choice of techniques used both for information-gathering and for eventual analysis. Three terms used to classify evaluation studies are applicable to the organizational consulting process as well (McDonald, 1993). These terms—bureaucratic, autocratic, and democratic—characterize the relationship of the consultant to the organization, which influences the kind of information that will be generated by the consulting process.

Bureaucratic consulting involves unconditional service to the agency. That is, the consultant is hired by the organization as an outsider and accepts the directions of those who hold the positions of power. The consultant has no independence and no control over how the information generated will be used; the main criterion of success is client satisfaction. Because the consultant's main relationship is with those in power within the organization, collaboration with workers is unlikely and the consultant remains an outsider. Most often this arrangement occurs within large bureaucratic organizations that are interested in internal reviews or interventions.

By contrast, an *autocratic* consultant is usually hired by, and responsible to, the government department that funds the social-service agency in question, either to evaluate it or to provide assistance with an organizational problem. In most cases the focus is on quantitative methods and standardized tests for assessing the organization. This process is termed 'autocratic' because the request for intervention comes from the funder of the service, not the service itself.

The consultant operating within a *democratic* arrangement is still an outsider in that she or he is hired—typically by the agency itself—to offer information and intervention services. The differences are that all workers are consulted, in confidence; the consultant and workers jointly come up with a plan of action; and the workers control the use of the information that is generated. In this collaborative endeavour, the outsider becomes to some extent an insider. According to Schein (1987), who refers to it as 'process consultation', this model is fundamentally an educational process for participants and consultant alike. It is seen as democratic because the contributions of workers are acknowledged along with those of the consultant.

Clearly the democratic approach offers the most straightforward opportunity for empowerment. Yet even autocratic or bureaucratic situations can provide learning opportunities for both organizations and consultants if power issues are analyzed carefully and questions of accountability are addressed with integrity. Kathleen McDermott (1987), for example, urges contract researchers to use the opportunity of an autocratic consulting context to study 'the culture of the powerful'. Through her own work as a consultant hired by the British government to evaluate a 'youth opportunities' program, she was able to reveal how the government used its power over the construction of youth unemployment and training to minimize resistance to a restructuring of the workforce that was not in the best interests of those with less power.

A useful perspective on the complexities of the consultant's position is provided by Stephanie Riger (1984) in a paper entitled 'On being on their side: Some difficulties in consulting with allies', in which she discusses some of the problems she encountered as a feminist who was initially perceived by feminist organizations as an outsider. Although she identified herself as a feminist, a consultant, and a researcher doing this work in order to contribute to the women's movement; as an outsider in academe by virtue of her interest in women's studies; and, finally, as someone who could help feminist organizations through the information collected in the consulting process, members of those organizations saw her as merely a representative of academe, someone whose findings could harm them, and who was not accountable to the organization itself. In this example she was operating from within an autocratic model, which did create contradictory allegiances. It is important, then, to clarify not only the type of consulting work that you are going to engage in but who you are accountable to. The dual locations held by the consultant, although often contradictory, can be combined with the perspectives of the members of feminist organizations to offer valuable insights throughout the consulting process that can be used to foster empowerment.

The following section will outline an interactive feminist model for a democratic consulting process that reflects my own background in community psychology, as a feminist service provider, as a researcher in the area of alternative social-service agencies, and as an organizational consultant.

AN INTERACTIVE FEMINIST CONSULTING PROCESS

An interactive feminist consulting process involves unpacking the internal and external relations of power within organizations and working with organizations to develop their work environments within an empowerment framework. In this model, the consultant has multiple roles (activist-consultant-researcher) and is able to 'use the tensions between the hyphens' to offer a particular viewpoint. A feminist consultant operates from a dual location as both 'insider' and 'outsider' to the feminist organization in question. She is an insider because she too identifies with the women's movement, shares the goals of the organization, and spends a period of time as a participant/collaborator within the organization, but she is also an outsider because her primary location is outside the organization, and her connection with the latter is only temporary.

The process outlined here consists of five stages: exploring organizational cultures; developing a critical analysis and action plan; intervening/transforming; reflecting and following-up; and considering the learning possibilities that the experience provides. Though the contract is limited, the process is set in motion and can continue within the organization with or without the consultant.

The consulting process documented here concerned a women's mental health clinic with which I worked some years ago. Because I had no intention of publishing an account of this work (and did not anticipate the rich store of information the process would produce), I did not ask for informed consent at the time—a request I now routinely make. To ensure anonymity and confidentiality, all identifying features of the organization have been removed, and some details have been changed.

Although this case was perhaps unusually tempestuous, it is particularly useful because of the range of issues it raises as well as the complexities it reveals: consulting is rarely a progressive, linear process. Following a brief history of the organization, I will outline the consulting process and discuss the issues that emerged at each stage.

Background

This privately funded women's mental health organization (WMHO) could be described as an alternative service agency. It had been operating since the mid-1980s, and as the services it offered had expanded so had the numbers of people on its staff. Much of their time and energy had been devoted to establishing the service. As is often the case with organizations that hire consultants, they felt that they were now at a point where they could begin working on internal organizational issues. In addition, there had been some friction between staff members, and a survey had been sent around to identify areas of tension. Generally, the survey found that staff wanted more input into the decisions that the administrator was making for the clinic. A decision was made then to hire a consultant to work with the staff on developing a new organizational model that would allow for greater worker participation and workplace democracy.

The organization consisted of a hierarchy of 20 paid staff: three full-time workers and the rest part-time and casual. The full-time workers were the administrator, an administrative assistant, and a counselling co-ordinator. Two medical doctors (the only men on staff), six counsellors (including three psychologists), four community nurses, and five office workers (all of whom had jobs elsewhere) made up the casual staff. There were also several volunteers who contributed to the running of the clinic.

When I was contacted to apply for the consulting contract, I was told that both the funds and the time available were limited (a typical feature in consulting work), but that the organization wanted someone to help it develop a mission statement that would reflect its feminist philosophy, a more democratic organizational structure, and a long-term plan for ongoing organizational development. My proposal outlining an interactive approach was accepted, and I began my work. The experience that followed illustrates the difficulties of creating participatory structures that satisfy the multiple contradictory and conflicting goals of variously positioned workers.

For each stage of the consulting process, I will first outline what happened in this particular case and then offer some broader commentary. It is worth noting that, in practice, the consultation process is rarely as progressive and rational as the 'stages' structure suggests: other organizational and interpersonal issues tend to surface that one cannot always be prepared for. These unanticipated moments provide additional opportunities for understanding life within organizations.

1. Exploring Organizational Cultures

My first step was to meet with the entire staff and go over the proposal I had submitted. The group agreed that I would facilitate two workshops: one to develop a mission statement and another to develop a new organizational structure. We also agreed that I would collect and review all of the organization's internal documents to get a sense of its history, and meet with all workers individually to get their input on the two goals of the consultation process. In addition, we established an advisory committee of seven representing the various staff categories (including the administrator), with whom I would meet to finalize the agenda for the workshops and to refine the process.

This step involves establishing trust and accountability. I needed both to explain my ways of working and to find out the staff's expectations for the consultation process.

Identifying problems

I then met individually with all 20 workers to learn about their particular work roles; their history with the organization; their ideas about a new structure; and the values that they wanted emphasized in the mission statement. The interviews, ranging in length from 45 minutes to two hours, were conducted on five separate days when all staff were on-site and appointments were fully booked. In this way I was able to get a sense of what the WMHO was like and how it operated at its busiest times.

This step was central to the effectiveness of the process. Listening to all the individuals within the organization and taking into account their varying locations helped to clarify the issues that they wanted addressed. I was able to compare the information I got from the interviews with the information from the survey that had been conducted by the organization. In addition, I was able to explain what could and what could not be addressed in the intervention that we were developing: for instance, that this was not a process of mediation that would resolve personality conflicts. This step was also important in establishing trust, as I had information about workers that they told me in confidence (the kind of information that cannot be used in a publication like this without informed consent). Listening to the experiences and expectations of the people involved, learning the historical and social context of the organization, and reading its internal documents and policies is all part of the process of unearthing the issues that need to be addressed.

2. Developing a Critical Analysis and Action Plan

I met with the advisory committee to share a summary of the information I had collected through individual interviews, document analysis, and the earlier survey asking for input on the focus of the consulting process. This discussion provided another opportunity to unearth and clarify issues. Overall, I was struck by the commitment of all the workers to engage in a process of change and to accept the will of the majority. Some felt more strongly than others about the need for a participatory structure, but all were ready to give the process a try. The staff, whatever their length of employment or job status, were willing to attend workshops without pay to foster organizational development. They also wanted to engage in group-building exercises stressing the common cause they shared through their work. Although all were proud of the services they provided, many also felt that they themselves needed to develop more trust interpersonally within the organization.

Three serious issues did emerge from my analysis of the interviews. First, some workers, unhappy with the private status of the clinic, wanted to explore the idea of becoming a non-profit worker co-operative; others, however, felt that such an arrangement would not be financially viable. Second, a number of workers were unhappy with the current administrator. They considered her ineffective, and part of the reason they wanted a new structure was in order to eliminate her position and her personal control over decision-making. Finally, some individuals saw the move for a participatory structure as coming from 'radical lesbian feminists' within the organization, who in their view were gaining control over it. Their concern was not with the idea of a participatory structure in itself, but with the degree of feminism that they perceived some of the lesbian workers to be advocating.

I raised each of these issues with the advisory committee. With respect to the first point, they made it clear that they did not wish me to address the organization's funding arrangements; they wanted to work on internal issues first, before exploring other options. They also discussed their reasons for wanting organizational change, and pointed out that it would be important to stress in the workshop that the aim would be to build a structure reflecting the values and philosophy of the agency, not those of the individuals currently working there. In other words, they acknowledged that some of the staff had conflicts with the administrator (a problem that the administrator herself was aware of). They felt that structural changes would help to reduce these interpersonal tensions. Finally, the 'radical lesbian feminist' issue was discussed in terms of varying degrees of feminist politics among staff members. We agreed that time would be needed to address the topic of feminism and its specific implications for the work of the WMHO. I agreed with the committee's decisions but was aware that there were underlying power issues that could surface at any time in the process. The ideological differences evident here point to the existence of multiple cultures within the organization.

This step requires that the consultant act as a facilitator to identify and address the areas of tension within the organization, most of which concern power and powerlessness. Identifying issues does not mean that the organization will always agree to address them; in this case, for instance, there was some reluctance to confront directly the homophobia that may have underlain some of the workers' concerns, although the committee was prepared to discuss this issue in terms of varying degrees of feminism. Moreover, consultants are contractually limited to working within the parameters originally defined by the organization. Nevertheless, we do have an ethical responsibility to raise the issues voiced as concerns by disempowered groups within the organization: in other words, to disrupt oppressive power structures. In a project evaluating battered women's shelters, Michelle Fine and Jaqui Wade (1986) confronted a similar problem. Fine (1992: 15) later wrote of this process:

> It took little genius to notice the whiteness of staff and residents. It required little insight to hear that the women's needs were not always compatible with their children's needs (as in the desire to see paternal grandparents). Our work was conceived as collaborative with shelters. Yet we ultimately generated what we considered to be important critical commentary—about race and racism and about children—which was not entirely shared by our collaborators.

Maintaining the dual location of insider–outsider is essential if the consultant is to produce a critical analysis and set a plan of action that can disrupt resistance to change.

3. Intervening/Transforming

The advisory committee and I finalized the agenda for the first workshop and circulated it among all staff members for their comments. The first session, which dealt with group-building and writing a mission statement, was a success. Workers came in with a commitment to improving their internal relations. The values of their organization were clear and agreed upon. They emphasized the importance of empowerment and choice in women's mental-health issues, they identified their work as political, and they stressed the need for consistency between philosophy, service provision, and organizational structure. A working group was struck to finalize the writing of the mission statement.

The second workshop, held two weeks later, focused on creating a participatory structure. Groups were asked to present their ideas for a new structure and, surprisingly, many similarities emerged. They envisioned a system of working teams that would operate co-operatively. Rather than one person in charge, there would be area teams with distinct tasks and responsibilities. However, despite this agreement, there was significantly more tension in this meeting than in the earlier one. In particular, the male doctors expressed concern about the efficiency of a participatory model and the amount of time it would take to make decisions. Others wondered how outside agencies would respond to working with an administrative team rather than a single individual. These issues were discussed until group agreement was reached. Again, a working committee was struck to begin to put this new structure into action and to ensure that all changes would be evaluated at regular intervals. An overall work plan was also agreed upon to determine the work that needed to be done, who would do it, and when. This workshop too was judged a success.

However, before the end of the formal eight-hour agenda, the administrator asked if people could stay longer because she had some issues to raise. Now following the principles of group decision-making, she wanted group agreement that money could be spent to send her to a mental-health conference. When asked about the current state of the budget, she was unable to provide detailed information, but then revealed that some staff members might have to be laid off. This was new and alarming information. The workshop ended with a new set of issues on the table that had not been captured by the original agenda for the organizational-change workshops.

I include this episode as part of the narrative because it reveals that interventions can bring about changes that the consultant does not anticipate. In this case, one positive surprise (the administrator's adoption of group decision-making) yielded a second, less positive one: disturbing new financial information that had tremendous implications for the process we were engaged in.

4. Reflecting and Following-up

Reflecting and following-up on the intervention process are critical both for the organization and for the consultant, to ensure that organizational development and renewal continue.

I met with the advisory committee a week later to follow up on the workshops, continue developing the new structure, and evaluate the consulting process. There was now some uncertainty about adopting a participatory management structure until the organization had sorted out its financial situation. The workshop, the timing of the consulting process, and the financial disclosure declaration made by the administrator were catalysts for much greater change. After meeting with the committee twice more, I saw, as they did, that they were unable to continue the process we had started. Some members of the staff had prevailed on a doctor in the clinic to ask the administrator to resign. My own role as consultant became very complicated. Although I was aware of some difficulties with the administrator, I tried to concentrate on the discrete task of creating a participatory work structure. However, power issues were emerging that raised interesting questions about the culture of the organization: Why was it one of the (male) doctors who was asked to talk to the administrator? How did the staff organize themselves to speak with one voice on this matter? At the same time, the resignation of the administrator brought uncertainty about adopting a participatory structure at all. Some of the women and one of the doctors thought she should be replaced, while others were more committed than ever to developing an alternative structure. Future meetings with me were cancelled. When a member of the WMHO called me to say that the consulting process was on hold, I was told that an internal staff member had taken over the administrative position. Nevertheless, the staff felt that in time they would implement their new structure, although the current state of the budget meant that they had to cut back on paid staff hours.

Four months later I resumed my work in the organization, which did eventually rewrite and achieve consensus on its mission statement and adopt participatory decision-making processes. The administration position was eliminated and administrative tasks were taken over by a two-person administrative team.

What might have been a straightforward 'empowering' intervention focusing on renewal and change revealed a complex and confusing set of power relations. This case study points to the value of viewing organizational culture through a critical postmodernist lens. In this instance, despite the organization's overall adherence to feminism, the ideological differences between individuals meant that the organizational culture was far from monolithic, and power relations were anything but static. The power relations between workers need ongoing deconstruction. This was an important lesson for me. No matter how many questions I ask or how much information I gather to plan an intervention, not everyone within an organization is going to be free to reveal everything they know and feel about their work; moreover, their position may change as the result of the interactive and reflective consulting process. Nor are all the consequences intended.

At the very least, writing an account of this process reveals the power relations that can emerge in dramatic and unforeseen ways when working for change. These unpredictable relations need to be included in the descriptive accounts used for research, for theorizing about organizational development and small group processes, and for building alternative organizations.

5. Learning Possibilities

The consulting process offers various learning possibilities, for both the organization and the consultant, that move beyond overly tidied descriptive accounts to more frankly troubled ones, and beyond the local problem-solving for which one is hired to the kind of critical analysis that contributes to social research.

About building alternative structures

The consulting process described here was intended to help one organization develop a participatory structure. But it also afforded learning opportunities that reinforced the findings of some of the research examining feminist movement organizations (FMOs) (Morgen, 1994; Riger, 1994; Ristock, 1987, 1990, 1991b). A couple of points stand out. First, even within alternative organizations, when difficulties arise some individuals will tend to fall back on ways that reflect bureaucratic rather than counter-bureaucratic thinking. This tendency was evident in the staff who turned to a doctor to ask the administrator to resign, in effect creating a power position that had never been intended as part of the clinic's structure, either before or after the proposed changes. Similarly, some staff wanted to replace the administrator, even though everyone had already agreed to work towards a less hierarchical structure. The fact that the doctor was one of only two men working in the organization suggests that gender may have played a role here as well.

Another tendency is for organizations to see different types of organizational structure as dichotomous and mutually exclusive (hierarchical and bureaucratic versus flat, non-bureaucratic). In this case, participatory management was seen as more 'feminist' than the traditional hierarchical arrangement. The problem with this construction is that it does not allow for consideration of the elements of dominant culture that can still be present even in 'alternative' structures. Organizational consultants must therefore resist recreating hegemonic cultures that ignore the oppressive power relations that can and do exist despite democratic structural changes. Attending to the specific power dynamics of the local site with a broader critical analysis of alternative structures in mind provided valuable insights into the difficulties and possibilities of building non-oppressive organizations.

About organizational cultures

Documenting the consulting process through critical case studies can enhance our understanding of organizations and provide a useful applied methodological approach for uncovering organizational 'cultures' (Ott, 1989): systems of shared values, interpretations, and assumptions (Frost et al., 1991). Feminist organizations are particularly important to such research because they are forming new organizational models and hence new cultures. Contrary to the standard view of organizations as closed systems in which workers' behaviours can be controlled and predicted, this case study reveals that in fact multiple cultures may be at play and interacting. Despite their shared mission statement and vision, the individuals within the WMHO were not homogeneous. Pointing out the contradictions and differences between these cultures is a first step towards learning to negotiate in such contexts. Analysis of organizational discourses can reveal how workplace practices are controlled through culture (Witten, 1993); in the case of the WMHO, for example, the discourse about 'radical lesbian feminists' may have served to keep lesbian workers in check. Research in the context of consulting can explore such links between discourses and power in their interactional contexts within the workplace (Witten, 1993).

About consulting as a research method

My work with the WMHO spanned approximately four months, during which I spent many hours within the organization. Such opportunities for collaborative work with communities are part of our empowerment project to build knowledge and change the conditions of people's lives. 'Being *in* the change' helped me to learn more about power and negotiation as processes. It is clear that feminist consultants cannot rely on a structural view of organizations but have to see the process of an empowerment intervention as political, involving shifts in and struggles for power (Riger, 1989). We have to acknowledge axes of difference such as gender, race, class, and sexuality, and their accompanying asymmetries of access to power, when we think about the social relations and culture of organizations. Among the questions that I would now consider central to organizational consulting are these: What are the discursive conditions that help to maintain organizational structures and work practices? How can we promote reflection and encourage people to see their multiple positionings within organizations? When do we stop intervening and start reflecting (Fine, 1992)? Are there ethical considerations, beyond confidentiality and safety, that consultants ought to take into account when we treat our work as research within a political movement (Riger, 1989)?

Reflections such as these point to the value of seeing particular, local efforts to bring about change as part of the broad process of social inquiry. The kind of feminist organizational consulting I have described here as one way of beginning research as empowerment can be extended to other kinds of work within organizations, such as program evaluation (see, for example, Mertens, Farley, Madison, and Singleton, 1994; Women's Research Centre, 1990) facilitating, and training. Anti-oppression training, which is currently being conducted for many feminist social-service agencies, is particularly important to document and to view within an empowerment framework. The challenge is to see the possibilities for uncovering knowledge that emerge in the course of working to 'unearth, disrupt and transform the existing institutional arrangements' of local sites. The following chapters explore these issues further, along with others that arise once a research project is under way.

4

Multiple Methods For Validity

When engaging in empowerment research, we are often struggling with the need for flexibility so that our research can emerge and evolve through our interactions with communities, while at the same time we are struggling to come up with a plan or research design that will help ensure that we can answer the questions that are central to our process of social inquiry. Being prepared to draw on multiple methods helps us to achieve flexibility. Choosing and assembling the appropriate ones is central to the value and integrity—the validity—of a research project. In this chapter I will draw on two examples to outline the use of multiple methods for research as empowerment.

In empowerment research we strive for reflexivity: that is, self-awareness. We try to be aware of how we observe and affect actions and discourse, and how we attribute meanings and intentions; of what understandings we are creating through the research project and how we are creating them (Reinharz, 1992; Wasserfall, 1993). In the literature of feminist and emancipatory research methodology, 'reflexivity' refers to self-consciousness with the goal of establishing non-exploitive relations between the researcher and the communities researched (Parker, 1992; Reinharz, 1992; and see Chapter 5). It is helpful to keep all these senses of 'reflexivity' in mind throughout the course of a research project, from design through implementation: reflecting on our own perceptions and decisions, on the aims and impact of our research, on the ways in which that research is and is not empowering. Reflexivity is closely tied to flexibility: being prepared to reshape the research design and adjust the research methods to reflect what we learn in the course of doing the research, both from the community and from our own reflections.

Some feminist researchers have suggested that qualitative methods are more consistent with feminist values than quantitative methods, while others have questioned the idea that there is one method that is most thoroughly feminist (Reinharz, 1993). Many feminists agree that no single research method, such as interviewing or surveying, is inherently feminist; what is important is how we use the methods in the research process and how we are informed by our theoretical framework (Reinharz, 1992). Postmodernist approaches share this concern for deconstructing the theory–method dichotomy and seek to make visible the 'processes of ideological construction of particular objects, and subjects, of inquiry' when 'gathering material' or 'collecting data' (Burman, 1992: 47). This kind of reflexivity, as Wasserfall (1993: 27) aptly notes, 'implies a distance and unity at once, and because of that, can make one aware of oneself as subject and object as well as of the process that creates the consciousness of both'. Although a reflexive mode can make for paralysis (see Chapter 2) in heightening our awareness of the limited, constructed nature of every statement, criterion, model, etc., empowerment research requires this double stance of 'unity and distance' as we facilitate research decisions and interactions that lead to action.

Among the guiding questions to be considered in choosing appropriate methods and ensuring reflexivity are these: What is the purpose of the project? In what context is the research being conducted? Whose interests are being served? Who benefits from this research? How can opportunities be taken that consider unanticipated questions, multiple perspectives and meanings? How can we best facilitate research as empowerment? Whose voices will be heard in this process? How can we acknowledge the contradictions that we uncover and still move ahead? (See also Rappaport, 1990.)

Working in an empowerment framework requires a research design that will draw attention to differences in power and help both to uncover dominant constructions and omissions and to articulate the experiences and perspectives of marginalized people; that will examine practices both of regulation within oppressive power relations and of resistance or agency; that will promote reflexivity and encourage action (Burman, 1992); that will encourage accountability and reciprocity, yet allow for various levels of collaboration with participants. We see these issues as critical to the validity of the research project.

VALIDITY

There are many conceptualizations of validity in traditional research (internal, external, discriminate, etc.). In general, validity pertains to methodology and signifies the degree to which the research design yields findings that provide an accurate picture of reality (Morawski, 1994) and are therefore-generalizable beyond the research sample. For many feminist researchers,

> **Validity:** the integrity and value of research; achieved through accountability both to the participants and to those who will be affected by the outcome.

however, the concept of validity reflects a different understanding of the nature of research findings and a different understanding of 'reality'. Generalizability of research findings is not a measure of validity for researchers who are critical of the universalizing and homogenizing tendencies of traditional approaches. Instead of asking whether the project design permits the researcher to uncover the truth, we ask how we can ensure that the research process has integrity. Our concern is not to bias the results in favour of a particular community, but to ensure that the information we gather will 'ring true'—that it will resonate with the experiences of participants—and that we are accountable both to them and to the broader communities that may be affected by our research. At the same time, accountability to research participants must not limit the researcher to presenting only affirmative findings. Since research as empowerment is almost by definition aimed at uncovering sexist, racist, classist, or otherwise oppressive uses of power, we may well find ourselves accountable to multiple audiences with conflicting interests. For example, a feminist researcher working on a day-care project may find that some women involved have a racist analysis of the needs of single mothers. Accountability to these participants would mean showing how our work has integrity and value by making our own critical analysis visible, not keeping it from them.

Patti Lather's (1991) articulation of three types of validity is useful here. *Construct validity* requires that we recognize and confront the theoretical traditions within which we are operating and be willing to challenge and change them; in other words, it demands flexibility in the research design. *Face validity* is related to construct validity; its purpose is to ensure that your work makes sense to others. It is achieved by checking your analyses, descriptions, and conclusions with at least some of the participants in your research; this is the kind of 'reality' check that is part of reflexivity. Finally, *catalytic validity* is achieved when participants, and the broader community affected by the research, feel energized or re-oriented in some way by the project. For research as empowerment this means that you have provided new understandings with strategic implications, or disrupted current ways of thinking about or responding to social issues. Underpinning our criteria for research 'validity', then, is our concern that research be 'valuable'.

Multiple Methods

Both Joan and I have relied on various methods, generating qualitative as well as quantitative data, in the course of our empowerment research. Using multiple methods (often referred to as triangulation) enables us to look at a subject from different angles and makes a study both richer and more reliable (Lather, 1991; Parlett and Hamilton, 1977). This process involves assembling multiple data sources and trying to assess the consistency as well as the 'counter patterns' (Lather, 1991) of findings across the varying modalities.

> **Triangulation:** using multiple methods in order to obtain more thorough coverage of a subject by viewing it from different angles. This can be achieved in two ways: by using different methods for different questions about the same topic, or by using different methods to explore the same set of questions.

In this chapter I describe two projects, both of which relied on multiple methods and thus permitted the dual process of affirmation and disruption that is part of our empowerment approach. In addition to discussing the choice of methods that goes into research design, this chapter will also examine issues such as project time frame, flexibility, and the reflexivity that is central to our concern for validity. It will also discuss what is achieved, how it is constructed and what is missed through the processes of data collection described.

RESEARCHING FEMINIST COLLECTIVES

My work on feminist social-service collectives began in 1987 as research for my Ph.D. dissertation. Having worked in collectives (primarily shelters) as a relief worker throughout graduate school, I wanted to describe and document their non-hierarchical democratic practices, an area that I felt had been ignored in academic literature on organizational structures, social movements, and group processes. At the same time I felt that in doing this research I would be working on behalf of feminist collective workers, some of whom had encouraged me and helped to shape my research questions. They wanted to know about other collectives in Canada, how they operated, and what problems they shared in common. Some also wanted research findings that would show funders that collective structures were viable for social-service delivery. At the time I undertook this research there were no Canadian studies documenting or examining the work of feminist social-service collectives. I wanted to explore the internal processes and difficulties associated with working collectively in order to document the actual work that was being done in Canada.

Although I was positioning myself as an advocate for collectives, my research design was directly shaped by the fact that I was working towards a graduate degree: not only did I have a time limit, and few resources, but I had to show the academy that this research was credible. I planned to consider three basic questions: What constitutes a collective? How did feminism influence their work? And, finally, did collectives perceive themselves as working for social change, in addition to their social-service work? The dual purpose of satisfying degree requirements and contributing to social change was a constant area of tension; (see Chapter 5) this was not necessarily a negative element, but it was one factor, among others, that influenced my motives and decisions as a researcher, and one that I needed to reflect on in the course of my work.

My research design had three components: a national survey of feminist social-service collectives; a content analysis of collective documents (such as service brochures and 'basis of unity' statements); and interviews with women working in four successful collectives. Combining these three methods made it possible to reflect critically on the work of feminist social-service collectives in Canada, in addition to documenting and describing it. The questionnaire provided a descriptive overview of feminist social-service collectives; the document analysis shed light on their public profile, as well as their values and goals, and finally, the interviews drew out the experiences of individual collective workers as well as their accounts of the culture of collectivity. (See Appendix I for these research instruments.)

Survey

The decision to use a questionnaire was based on the need to reach as many collectives as possible within a limited budget. In designing it, I tried to ensure that it would not take too much time to complete, but would also stimulate reflection on the part of respondents. The result was a questionnaire that asked about their internal processes of self-defined feminist social-service collectives; the difficulties associated with working collectively; how feminism has influenced their work and organizational structure; and respondents' perceptions of how their work contributed to social change.

To identify self-defined feminist social-service collectives I contacted provincial and national feminist organizations such as the National Action Committee for the Status of Women, provincial coalitions of sexual assault and rape crisis centres, provincial Status of Women action groups, and the Ontario Association of Interval and Transition Houses, as well as women's bookstores across the country, and asked them for the names of such agencies in their areas. The 67 organizations identified were then contacted by telephone to verify that they defined themselves as feminist social-service collectives. Through these telephone calls, I found that the service mandate of most of the collectives in this sample fell under the category of services in response to violence against women. Thus most of the collectives were rape crisis centres, sexual assault centres, shelters for battered women, and emergency transition hostels. This new information helped to shape some of the questions that I would later explore.

Questionnaire

The 30 items that made up the questionnaire were based primarily on a review of the literature and my previous experience working in collectives. The questionnaire included both forced-choice and open-ended items. As a check for the appropriateness and clarity of items, and for face validity, I asked three members from different collectives to examine the questionnaire, with the result that small changes were made in the wording of some items. A cover letter explaining the purpose of the research study asked for participants' signed consent, as well as any documents that would provide a fuller understanding of the agency (e.g., basis of unity statements, informational brochures, etc.). To encourage a prompt response, follow-up telephone calls were made to all agencies one month after the questionnaires were mailed out.

The survey proved useful in providing a broad picture of where collectives were located across the country, the kinds of work they did, how long they had been in existence, and the strengths and difficulties associated with the collective structure. The high response rate indicated that respondents saw this research as valuable and wanted to know what I was learning from other collectives. As a research tool, the questionnaire was clearly working as I had designed it to, constructing the voices of collectives as a response to the academic literature in which I felt there were serious omissions and misconceptions about collective structures. However, by firmly basing the questions on the assumptions of this academic literature, I was missing a full exploration of some areas that had not yet been explored. For example, because the academic literature characterized the collective structure as inefficient for social-service delivery, I asked questions designed to challenge that view by exploring benefits other than efficiency, and goals of social transformation, not just social service. But I did not address issues, such as identity politics, that were not suggested, directly or indirectly, by that literature. With respect to its construct validity, then, the questionnaire was not as flexible as it might have been.

Document Analysis

The documents that the collectives returned with their questionnaires were primarily informational brochures describing the organizations' services and practices. Some collectives also sent vision and philosophy statements. Clearly all these were public rather than internal documents. Their common emphasis on feminist values suggested that it would be useful to undertake a formal analysis of the values and goals contained in these documents. More specifically, I was looking for the presence of values or concepts that would confirm the existence of an alternative feminist approach to social change and service delivery. I developed a rating instrument based, in part, on the results of an open-ended item in the questionnaire asking why their organization works collectively, which consistently indicated that four values were central: empowerment, equality, sharing, and social change.

Although this document analysis was planned from the start, it was only after reading the materials provided that I realized they would allow for assessment of the consistency with, and counter-patterns to, the values that respondents had described in the questionnaire as being central to their work. The rating sheet was divided into three sections, each consisting of a number of items that could be checked off to indicate the presence of particular goals or concepts:

A. Stated goals: assessing whether collectives stated any broader social-change goals, in addition to fulfilment of their service mandate. Three specific goals could be checked off: empowerment, equality, and social change.

B. Processes stated: assessing qualitative difference in the services offered that might reflect specifically feminist values. Four specific processes could be checked off: women helping women, sharing, choice, and non-judgemental services.

C. Definition of services: assessing whether the documents indicated that the agency defined itself as a collective; operated with a feminist ideology; and/or addressed the issue of violence against women.

In addition, each section included an open-ended item in which other goals, processes, and definitions of services could be recorded. The documents provided by each collective were read by myself and one other person, after which we would independently fill out the rating sheet. The fact that we reached 100 per cent agreement indicated that the documents were straightforward in their presentation of values, and that the categories developed to analyze the documents were appropriate.

The document analysis was an attempt to verify the existence of certain values. The limitation of this approach is that it may serve merely to confirm what is already explicit (in this case, the values that the collectives officially stated) rather than to explore less obvious issues (such as values that might be implicit, or conflicting in some way) (Parker, 1992). At the time, for example, I did not analyze what was not said, an approach I would now include in this process. Nevertheless, the document analysis was a useful way of exploring questions from a different angle than that provided by the questionnaire. Were the values the collectives reported to me consistent with those they presented to the public? What kinds of services were they attempting to build? These questions were reflected in the interview question about the contradictions that collective workers experienced in their work. The link between ideology and structure was another issue that I was able to explore in more detail through interviews.

Interviews

Whereas the survey and document analysis provided big-picture information about how collectives operated and presented themselves to the public, the interviews permitted in-depth exploration of the experiences and perceptions of the women working in these agencies and made it possible to obtain a more critical view of the collective structure than was likely to show up in mission statements and formal documents. In my informal conversations with collective workers before starting the research project, I had learned of the struggles of women's groups to retain this organizational form. It became important to me to find out 'what worked' in those collectives that had been in existence for a long time, and how they had grown and changed. I also looked for agencies that had developed variations within their collective structure (such as specialized work roles and teams, satellite collectives, and subdivision into groups and caucuses) and that indicated a connection between their feminist ideology and their collective structure.

I was able to identify several such collectives in various regions of Canada on the basis of the questionnaire and document analysis, but financial constraints meant that interviews were restricted to the Toronto area; although limiting, this was not inconvenient, given my previous work history in collectives there. I telephoned four collectives and asked to interview any two workers who were willing to participate, with one proviso: since the results from the questionnaire indicated that tensions sometimes arise between long-time and newer collective members, in each case I asked that one of the interviewers be an 'old' collective member (more than five years' service) and one a 'new' member (less than three years' service).

I interviewed each worker separately for approximately one and a half hours and tape-recorded the sessions (except for one in which the participant preferred that I write down her responses). Each interview was structured around a set of questions exploring themes suggested by the responses to the questionnaire and the document analysis; they included personal reasons for working collectively, strengths of collective structure, difficulties experienced in collective work, contradictions experienced, issues related to diversity and tension, visions for self in this work, and goals and visions for the organization. In all instances the interviews became dialogues, following a constructive, interactive model (Oakley, 1981).

Although my initial intention had been to explore what made successful collectives work, the interviews also revealed other aspects of collective culture, particularly the tensions, contradictions, and difficulties that can arise because of differences in sexuality, class, race, and age, as well as experience with collective structures. Clearly racism, homophobia, and classism existed within these collectives despite their ideological emphasis on unity. Exploring such power differentials in interviews helped me to develop my own critical analysis so that I could defend the viability of collective structures and at the same time interrogate the dominant view within many collectives that this was a structure by definition consistent with a feminist analysis of violence against women (Ristock, 1993).

In summary, my research journey was a reflexive process of triangulating methods in response to findings as I proceeded. The national survey provided necessary descriptive information—a snapshot of what was happening across Canada; the document analysis provided insights into the public profile of collectives and the strong link between feminist values and the collective structure; and the interviews elicited personal accounts that provided in-depth and critical information about the contradictory and complex culture of collectives. Overall, the project revealed that collectives were both viable and contradictory. It also clarified the way in which collectivity is constructed, thereby encouraging efforts to deconstruct and resist hegemonic tendencies while promoting efforts to create and shape democratic organizational forms. Using multiple methods with a reflexive process made it possible to uncover and affirm the work of feminist social-service collectives while disrupting any fixed ideal of collectivity.

Reflections

The project described here had, of course, many limitations. Since this research was part of my work towards a Ph.D., academic requirements played an important part in determining my approach. I was committed to an empowerment framework to the extent of consulting with participants and exploring questions that were of interest to them, not just to me; I conceived of this research as contributing to feminist efforts to invent non-oppressive organizational structures; and I believed that documenting the work of collectives would contribute to social action by allowing other groups access to information that would benefit their own organizing efforts. Nevertheless, at the time neither the literature on feminist research and postmodernism nor my own sense of what research as empowerment meant was as complete as it would later become. I would perhaps make different choices now in my research design and development of research instruments. For instance, the questionnaire was too abstract; in not considering the social context or historical developments that had led these agencies to adopt a collective structure—that is, in failing to attend fully to the specifics of local situations—it did not permit an adequate analysis of power. Being derived mainly from the literature I was dissatisfied with, the questions themselves did not put collective workers' experiences at the centre of the research and thus may have missed important features of collective work that had yet to be addressed in the literature. The information gained was descriptive and based on individual perceptions that may not have reflected the views of the entire collective. Similarly, the document analysis was limited by its reliance on established categories, which may have obscured other values and reflected my own interest in specific features. Finally, while the interview component provided some insight into the social context and the historical development of the four enduring collectives examined, the information gained did not represent the full range of voices of collective workers, leaving me to wonder what those who were not interviewed would have said.

These limitations reflect common practical difficulties in developing an empowering research design. Constraints of time and resources, coupled with a desire for useful results, mean that a project often has to be limited: not everyone can be interviewed, and certain questions are not asked. Given these limitations, however, the research can still be held to standards of integrity, value, and accountability. This account of my research on collectives shows that I assembled varying data sources using several different methods. Even with limited research funds (a doctoral fellowship) and a degree-driven time frame, there was time to use multiple methods and reflect the input of participants; it took approximately one year to complete the survey, document analysis, and interviews, in that order. After completing each step I was able to reflect on the next one and alter my original plans in order both to incorporate the information I had gathered and to attempt to gather counter-information.

The fact that this study has led me to additional research and involvement with feminist social-service agencies is an indication of its catalytic validity. I have shared information from my work with developing collectives, helped organizations to network with one another, and presented my research at community conferences in addition to academic forums; doing the research equipped me to write 'basis of unity' and personnel documents for collectives, with which I continue to work (often as a consultant) to find new ways of maintaining and creating consistency between feminist philosophies and organizational structures (see Chapter 3).

Though I took research participants seriously and my work was shaped in response to what they told me, this design was one that I alone, more or less, controlled. The next example indicates how multiple methods and the demands of collaborating with many stakeholders bring forward new ideas in research design. I have become more flexible in the empowerment research process because of feminist and postmodernist influences that reinforce the importance of reflecting on how we are constructing the process of social inquiry.

RESEARCHING LESBIAN ABUSE

The following example of research on abuse in lesbian relationships illustrates the value of a flexible research plan that can change shape and direction in response to information gathered from participants in the course of the research. For the last six years I have been actively involved in a major research program aimed at understanding abuse in lesbian relationships and working with social-service agencies, friends, families, and lesbian communities to develop appropriate intervention strategies. This is an area where very little research has been done to date, in part because lesbians disagree as to whether it is productive or even safe to address this problem in the context of mainstream academic or government-funded projects. Given the high stakes (the potential for increasing the negative stereotyping of lesbians versus the danger of continuing to deny the existence of such abuse), it has been crucial to work with reflexivity and accountability to the communities affected by this research. The following account of the evolution of my research design details my attempts to achieve the three types of validity that we have identified as central to research as empowerment.

My work in this area began when I volunteered at the Toronto Counselling Centre for Lesbians and Gays. Laurie Chesley, Donna MacAulay, and I received a grant from the Ontario Women's Directorate to conduct a survey of lesbian communities in Toronto aimed at determining the prevalence of lesbian abuse, the kinds of abuse experienced, and community responses to the abuse, in order to start a counselling group for survivors. Having distributed 500 questionnaires to lesbians in Toronto, we received a second grant from the Directorate to produce a handbook based on our research and work with clients that was then distributed to social-service agencies throughout Ontario, including shelters for battered women, women's resource centres, and services for lesbians and gays (Chesley, MacAulay, and Ristock, 1991). Although the booklet was intended for an Ontario audience, so many requests for it came in from across Canada that a second printing was required. This response confirmed the importance of continuing this work in hopes of answering some of the questions that feminist writings on violence against women do not seem able to answer.

After moving to Winnipeg in 1990 I began an interview research project, which is ongoing, in which I am attempting to put lesbians' experiences of violence at the centre of the process by asking participants to describe their experiences. At the same time I am engaging in discourse analysis, assessing the interviews as accounts/texts that indicate how lesbians are constructing their experiences through feminism, counselling, 12-step programs, and so on. The two primary goals are to address the barriers to service provision that lesbians face and to advance non-heterosexist theorizing of violence against women through discourse analysis. Focusing on language and ideologies helps draw attention to how we make meanings out of experiences and, in this case, how violence is in part discursively constructed, experienced, and perceived through the filter of heterosexist thinking. The qualitative in-depth information acquired in these interviews will be compared and contrasted with the results of the larger survey research project that was undertaken in Winnipeg and Toronto. Overall, my aim is to contribute to the development of feminist theories on violence through a critique of the assumptions in current gendered theories of violence that reflect heterosexual dynamics. Disruption of grand-narrative theorizing on violence and affirmation of lesbians' experiences are at the centre of this work—a more postmodern perspective and methodology than in my research on collectives. Recently I had the opportunity of expanding this research into more immediate action when I undertook a needs assessment in order to develop anti-homophobia training for shelter and second-stage housing workers providing services to survivors of domestic abuse.

Training and Education: The CLOSE Project

In 1992 a group of lesbian service providers concerned about abuse in lesbian relationship (Coalition of Lesbians on Support and Education, or CLOSE) were meeting in Winnipeg to discuss a range of issues having to do with homophobia and heterosexism in social services. Although, as a committee of like-minded people, in a sense we formed an 'inclusive community', we by no means undertook to 'include' all the differences of opinion that exist within lesbian communities—differences revolving around issues such as the danger of feeding a homophobic discourse, addressing abuse within lesbian communities before involving mainstream services, and how to work with lesbian abusers—much less to resolve them. This is not to say that we were prepared to act unilaterally as the voice of lesbians; in fact, a major feature of our plan was to consult with as diverse a group of lesbians as we could. However, all of us had been involved in such debates for years, and we felt it was time to respond to some of the immediate needs of abused lesbians. Had we delayed action until all these issues had been resolved, or had we been a more divided, diverse group, a project like this might never have advanced beyond the discussion stage.

We applied for and received funding for a one-year project called Training and Education: Responding to Abuse in Lesbian Relationships.[1] The first stage of this project entailed conducting a needs assessment of lesbians and of shelter and second-stage housing workers around the issues of homophobia and heterosexism, barriers to service provision, and, more specifically, abuse in lesbian relationships. In the second stage, building on the findings of the needs assessment, we designed and implemented a training program for shelter and second-stage housing workers throughout Manitoba.

Research Design

Needs assessments are often criticized by community members as time-consuming and redundant activities, revealing information that is already known and thereby delaying or neutralizing necessary action. We[2] believed that in this case the needs assessment itself could be educational and empowering and could help us to produce a training package that would be responsive to the needs both of lesbians and of shelter and second-stage housing workers.

On the one hand, it was important to assess the needs of lesbian communities across Manitoba to identify the gaps and barriers in social-service provision both generally and specifically with respect to lesbian abuse. On the other hand, we also had to meet the needs of the shelter and second-stage housing workers charged with responding to lesbian abuse. Expecting resistance, we felt it was necessary to consult and collaborate with both communities in order to gain their support for our project. Thus we separated the needs assessment into two parts, using different approaches because of the differences between these constituencies.

Lesbian communities

To research lesbian communities throughout Manitoba we had to come up with a design that would reach as many people as possible. We wanted to understand differences in experiences based on geographic location (urban, rural, northern) as well as race, age, religion, ability, and class. Given the ways in which homophobia keeps lesbians invisible, silent, and closeted, this was not an easy task. We needed a design that would be sensitive to this complicated context. We were interested in two main questions: what their experiences had been with social services, both generally and specifically with reference to lesbian abuse, and what they would ideally like to see developed in the way of services and support systems. To address these central questions we relied on a combination of focus groups, questionnaires, and individual interviews. (See Appendix II.)

Focus groups brought lesbians together to discuss and share their experiences. In addition to contacting established groups—gay and lesbian youth groups, a Jewish lesbian group, two-spirited people (aboriginal gays and lesbians)—we made announcements in various social settings inviting lesbians to a forum. Participants met in small discussion groups with facilitators who tape-recorded and summarized on flip charts the responses to our questions. In addition to giving us important information, this method allowed for consciousness-raising about the issue of lesbian abuse and provided an opportunity for lesbians in various areas to learn about our project and perhaps organize a response themselves to the barriers and issues identified in their communities.

At the same time we realized that not all lesbians would feel comfortable or able to come to group meetings, so we also left *questionnaires* at bars, community agencies, and bookstores, which could be filled out anonymously, asking the same questions posed in the focus groups. Finally, to provide lesbians with an opportunity to speak more personally about their experiences, we placed advertisements in newspapers with a 1-800 phone number inviting lesbians from across the province to call us. Telephone *interviews* were conducted using the same questions that were asked in the survey and focus groups.

Triangulation—using three different approaches to ask the same questions—maximized our opportunities to reflect geographic and cultural diversity, giving a voice to lesbians throughout Manitoba, and facilitated the assessment of both commonalities and counter-patterns in the responses. This process has also contributed to my own interview research project as it let more people know of my work and allowed them to meet me, which may have made some women feel more comfortable about calling to arrange interviews.

Service providers

The needs assessment for the shelter and second-stage housing workers first involved meeting with representatives of the Manitoba Association of Women's Shelters (MAWS) in order to gain their support and give them an opportunity to suggest a method that they would find suitable for their work environment. We also wanted to ensure that rural and northern shelters, including those on First Nations reserves, would be able to participate. Based on the feedback from MAWS, we decided on telephone interviews at pre-arranged times to go over a questionnaire that would be sent in advance. This approach was time-limited (interviews were scheduled for one and a half to two hours) and did not require travel, but allowed for a conversational format that was more personal than a survey. Where possible, we tried to interview both an administrator and a front-line worker at each shelter, since their perspectives might reflect their different roles. Extra questionnaires were sent to shelters and second-stage houses, in case individual workers wanted to express their views.

In consultation with MAWS, we developed a series of questions that would help us to understand the context of the work of shelters and help respondents to reflect on their work environment. Some questions asked about funding sources and governance structure, existing policies on anti-discrimination, whether their mandate included lesbians, and whether they had had any training about homophobia. Many questions focused on lesbian abuse and the respondents' understandings and questions about this issue. But we also felt we needed to ask general questions about their knowledge of issues facing lesbians, including lesbian workers. We wanted to maintain a connection between the larger context of lesbians' lives (including homophobia and heterosexism) and abuse in lesbian relationships. This approach proved to be successful because of the collaborative work done with the MAWS people and their awareness and input into the development of the questionnaire.

Reflections

This research project was successful in identifying many of the barriers that lesbians face in trying to gain access to services that are often limited by homophobia. As is often the case with needs assessments, much of this information was perhaps predictable. Nevertheless, this project was not just another 'needs assessment that doesn't touch the need': it allowed lesbians to come together and share their concerns, and in raising their collective awareness it may have helped some to mobilize within their communities. Our emphasis on training (a form of action) also allowed us to give shelter and second-stage housing workers an insight into lesbian issues that in many cases had been lacking. This gave our project value and credibility within lesbian communities. The steps of the needs assessment—bringing some lesbians together in focus groups, soliciting the involvement of others through questionnaires and newspaper advertisements; consulting with shelter and second stage-housing workers and interviewing someone from every shelter in Manitoba—made for a flexible consultative process that ensured the project's validity on all three counts (construct, face, catalytic) and that brought together counter-patterns for us to analyze (the experiences of lesbians and the experiences of shelter workers). The needs assessment proved to be a pedagogical tool. Agencies that might have resisted anti-homophobia training (claiming they did not need it) welcomed training on another form of violence. By the time they had participated in our telephone interview they were open to a three-day workshop on lesbian abuse that focused largely on homophobia and heterosexism. In sum, then, even though many of the needs were known to us from the outset, the needs assessment served an important educational function and was, in fact, a political gesture resulting in a number of significant consequences.

Yet our intentions are not the only ones shaping and controlling the research process. Receiving government funding meant that we were on the government's timetable. We had one year for the entire project and were obliged to finish the needs assessment relatively quickly. We also had to gear more of our efforts to training within shelters than to work within lesbian communities because the former was seen as the more 'fundable' activity (for more on funding issues see Chapter 7). There is much to be done within lesbian communities in terms of education, political mobilizing, organizing to set up new and needed services, and so on, but these activities are not funded by the government. Part of our reflexive analysis, clearly, must include an examination of what was left out of this research design and what remains hidden. We can address this by exploring how we have been positioned in this project by government funders, lesbians, and shelter workers, and how we have positioned ourselves; and can look to disrupt these locations and their constraining effects.

Working in the area of lesbian abuse within social services is a politically charged activity. Many lesbians are rightly fearful that open discussion of this issue will subject them to even more homophobia, while feminist service providers often feel that addressing this issue will fuel the backlash against recognizing violence against women as a political issue by enabling right-wingers to say 'See, women are violent too.' (See Chapter 7.) We believe that the research process outlined here does what Michelle Fine (1992: 21) describes as 'unfreez[ing] moments of problematic political decision-making'. The research helped shelters and lesbians to unravel some of the contradictions and dilemmas they faced in addressing the issue of abuse in lesbian relationships. The research design allowed for an empowering collaborative process that disrupted dominant discourses on violence and lesbians in the interest of social action.

Conclusions

This chapter has provided two examples of research projects that used multiple methods to gather data. Each shows the importance of context (why you are doing the research and who you are doing it for) in determining the research design. The examples also show the need for flexibility and creativity. One approach to triangulation is to ask new and different questions with each method, as I did in the project on collectives; the other is to ask the same questions using different methods, as we did in the project on lesbian abuse. In order to be responsive to research participants, we have to be willing to shift our original intentions and come up with new ways and more ways of allowing voices to come forward. Our research designs must also allow us to work towards social action while uncovering new understandings about our research areas, always being aware that we are constructing a narrative whose content—both what it includes and what it omits—reflects our particular choice of research design. These features give validity to research within an empowerment framework. But Michelle Fine (1992: 219) also reminds us of the power relations that operate even when we are bringing forward multiple voices. She writes:

> . . . researchers mystify the ways in which we select, use, exploit voices. That we use them, I am delighted. That we fail to articulate how, how not, and within what limits is a failure of methodology and a flight from our own political responsibilities to tell tough, critical, and confusing stories about the ideological and discursive patterns of inequitable power arrangements.

The following chapter will explore some of the ways in which power operates throughout the research process, focusing on the relationship between the researcher and the researched and emphasizing self-reflexive analysis as an essential component of empowerment research design.

Notes

[1] CLOSE members oversaw the project and contributed directly by providing input and feedback on the needs assessment; planning and facilitating the training. CLOSE members include Liz Adkins, Blu Peppas, Lynne Pinterics, Janice Ristock, Sharon Taylor,

and Lee Woytkiw. KLINIC Community Health Centre was the organizational sponsor for this project, which was funded by the Family Violence Prevention Division, Health Canada (Project# 4887-07-93-011).

[2] Gerry Pearson was the paid project co–ordinator who was primarily responsible for the lesbians' needs assessment while Angie Balan was the paid project coordinator responsible for the shelter/second-stage housing workers' needs assessment. Rhonda Chorney was hired on contract to provide data analysis services. I was the principal investigator who oversaw the needs assessment and met weekly with project staff to develop and oversee the process. Staff and CLOSE members worked collaboratively on the project as a whole.

5

Power Plays

However successfully we manage to adhere to the principles of empowerment, and however hard we strive to avoid the errors we have learned to recognize as abuses of confidentiality and other risks of harm to participants, there is no getting away from issues of power. Power gets played out in the funding of the research, in the participants' decision to participate, in the interactions between the researcher and the researched, in the way the data are interpreted, and in the use that is made of them. Moreover, both researcher and participants bring with them social histories of race, class, gender, sexuality, age, and other power-associated differences in social position that reverberate throughout their interaction, whether the researcher pays attention to them or not. Feminist researchers, though, tend to be particularly aware of these power issues, especially in cases where the researcher belongs to a dominant social category relative to the research participants. Even the requirement that university researchers obtain the approval of a research ethics committee is a recognition of the potential for some kinds of misuse of power to occur in the research process. But beyond the province of such committees is a whole range of power issues that the researcher must be attentive to. These power issues are not inherently negative; nor are they neutral. They are complex and contradictory interactions that shape what can be uncovered in the research process. Examining these 'microphysics of power' in research (Foucault, 1977) is necessary if we are to understand both the interpersonal and the structural relations that affect the research process.

Consciousness of our own locations, our subjectivities, and the narratives we construct about the work we are engaged in is a key component of research as empowerment, for these affect the ways in which we negotiate the social interactions involved in research. But detailed examinations of power plays are rarely considered part of the serious business of collecting data, nor are they likely to be included, where they logically could be, in the methodologies sections of reports on community-based research. Instead, we are most often given a sanitized view of the research process, which can result in an almost romantic story of its outcomes. In keeping with their general disdain for autobiographical work, many academics consider self-reflexivity a self-centred, even unseemly, variety of navel-gazing that diverts attention from the point of the research to the interior life of the researcher. On the contrary, the purpose of self-reflexivity is to improve the quality of research, not to derail it. Clarity about power issues is particularly important in community-based research, where researcher–participant interaction is often intense and research outcomes are expected to serve as bases for action. Self-reflexivity can show us areas in our data analysis and conclusions that are not accounted for in even the best-laid plans for community action research.

> **Power plays** arise because of tensions between the researchers' subjectivities and the demands of social relations encountered in the research process. They are made visible through adherence to the principle of reflexivity in writing accounts of the research process.

Attention to the microphysics of power points to areas of tension that, left unexamined, might misdirect our analysis. For instance, Kathleen Rockhill (1987) describes both the difficulty and the importance of bringing our subjectivities into the work we do. Re-examining transcripts of interviews from a research project that she was engaged in years earlier on literacy programs for immigrant Hispanic women, Rockhill writes, she was appalled by the violence in their lives but even more alarmed by the fact that she had not considered the information relevant to her questions about literacy in everyday lives:

> I had made the conscious choice to downplay the violence because I did not want to perpetuate and contribute to negative, class-biased racist stereotypes about the Mexican community. . . . As I worked it fell into place, and I saw that far from being peripheral to the problem of literacy in their lives, the violence that women experienced was central (Rockhill, 1987: 15).

Rockhill's re-analysis of her research project points to the potential interference of the microphysics of power: in this example, the power of the researcher to determine what is and what is not significant in interview transcripts. In reviewing the transcripts, Rockhill used her own subjectivity (in this case her own experiences of violence) as part of the base of her inquiry and could now see the power dynamics that, without her knowledge, had originally framed her research project and shaped her analysis.

In the context of research, then, the old feminist slogan 'the personal is political' means that we must start from the personal and indicate the ways in which our locations and identities as researchers inform and shape the research process. Sandra Harding (1987) and others have noted the difficulties facing feminist researchers who take this approach, among them the contradictions in our identities that we may experience: for example, tensions between our identities as women and our identities as academic researchers. Overall, though, the message is an encouraging one: that these 'fragmented identities' can be 'a rich source of feminist insight' (Harding, 1987: 8) if we make the effort to understand how they inform the research process—an effort that Liz Stanley and Sue Wise (1983; 1993) have referred to as 'intellectual autobiography' and, more recently, the 'research labour process'.

This process itself is not without potential pitfalls. For example, there has been a tendency to list the locations informing the research process in terms of identity (race, class, and sexuality). Although this allows the reader to understand who is doing the work, it can lead to debates over who can and should conduct research on certain topics. Renate Klein (1986) suggests that we cannot speak *for* others, but can and must speak *out* for others. Any concern with social beings and social issues, therefore, must also involve a sensitivity to the power issues that influence and shape the research (Oakley, 1991). More recently, Kum-Kum Bhavnani (1994: 34) has argued that 'the micropolitics of the research situation need to be analyzed, and not only noted'. What we want to avoid is feeling satisfied that we have adequately located ourselves when we have merely listed the social and identity groups to which we belong. Research as empowerment strives to explore the contingent and variable sense of self that postmodernists refer to as subjectivity as a way of analyzing the power relationships in research.

The account that follows reveals the difficulties I have experienced in attempting to satisfy Klein's (1986) demand for 'transparency in all stages of our research'. Although feminists have not ignored these difficulties, many of the barriers and contradictions experienced in the research process have not been fully acknowledged. In this chapter, then, I first reflect on the problems I have encountered in conducting feminist research, the often unacknowledged difficulties involved in achieving the goal of 'transparency—making visible why we do what we do—and how we do this' (Klein, 1986: 14) that is part of an empowerment paradigm. Returning to the project on feminist social-service collectives described in Chapter 4, I focus on what I have come to see as the inherent struggles involved in the 'knowledge/power couplet' (Walkerdine, 1990) that influences our research choices and interactions. Reporting the influences and contradictions of our multiple locations (in this case, my locations as researcher, academic, feminist, activist, and lesbian) is often necessary if we are to appreciate the complexity—methodological, epistemological, and political—of doing feminist empowerment research. In the second half of the chapter I reflect on my ongoing interview project on lesbian abuse as an example of the structural obstacles that are often present in attempts to construct knowledge about marginalized and disenfranchised groups. Here the focus is on strategic ways of negotiating power relations. Instead of denying or ignoring areas of tension in our work, we must learn how to anticipate, think through, negotiate, and work with power as a way of enriching the research process and maintaining its integrity.

RESEARCHER–RESEARCHED RELATIONSHIPS

Even before starting my research on feminist social-service collectives, I was well aware of several limitations that affect most research projects: I could not address all the issues that might emerge; there would undoubtedly be problems along the way; and underlying the entire process would be the tension between my dual locations as a feminist activist and a feminist academic. Yet even when I had acknowledged these limitations, I was still not entirely prepared for what I have come to see as one of the most sensitive issues in conducting feminist research: that is, the nature of the relationship between the researcher and the researched.

As feminists we have been aware of the unequal power and the exploitative potential inherent in this relationship (Harding, 1987). We struggle to develop new methodologies and meta-theories to circumvent the 'power-over' kind of research relationship: we state our goals in terms of empowerment; we treat our research participants with respect and equality; we locate ourselves within the questions we ask; we seek to make our research socially useful; we adhere to ethical guidelines that require reflexive feedback, informed consent, and no use of deception. But the issue of power remains, regardless of our attempts at sisterhood, thoughtfulness, and sensitivity. Power is always present in the complex reciprocal relationship between the researcher and the research participant. We cannot deny this power, nor can we deny the contradictions we experience between our roles as researchers and as women. As Gouldner (1971) suggests, alternative research must be reflexive, acknowledging the researcher as both 'knower' and 'discoverer'.

A web of power relations becomes visible in the research process when we pay attention to these roles. During the first phase of this project, I would often feel immobilized and unsure of my responsibilities as a researcher because of the power I felt this role gave me and my own discomfort with it. At times I experienced guilt and resentment over the bind I felt I was in, although at other times I felt satisfied with the work itself. This range of feelings made it clear to me that many feminist discussions of research have yet to describe fully the complexity of power and struggles with subjectivity in research. Celia Kitzinger (1991) has written about the paradox of power in feminism. She is critical of oversimplifications that suggest that male power is bad and female power good; or that power is neutral, and what matters is how you use it. She argues that we need a theory of power. Examining the feelings that arise in the course of research is one way to begin to theorize power by incorporating our insights into our analyses. In practical terms, this means being honest with ourselves, reflecting on the actions we take and attending to the range of emotions we experience throughout the research process. It also means putting these reflections into a balanced perspective that allows us to acknowledge that some of our experiences are relatively harmless aspects of the inevitably complicated process of working with other people, while others point to problem areas that might threaten research integrity, and others still reflect unanticipated issues and gaps in our current thinking about the work we are engaged in. My reflections on the power plays I experienced in researching feminist collectives are offered here as an example of the issues normally ignored in research reports. While these experiences occurred several years ago, when I was perhaps a less seasoned researcher, I do not feel they should be glossed over as mere instances of 'inexperience' associated with a developmental stage from which researchers graduate. As my thesis supervisor, Jeri Dawn Wine, said of another such issue, 'Pay attention to it now because you might not be able to see it in a few years.' Often we do not so much resolve these issues as become more accustomed and, regrettably, less sensitive to them.

Power Plays

In my research on collectives, each step required women to share their thoughts and feelings; to reflect on and evaluate their work; to take risks and trust me as a researcher. In this respect I felt that the process succeeded quite well. Return rates were high and I had little difficulty finding women to interview and gaining access to information. But the very fact that I gained such access indicates that I had power, and while power is not always misused, recognizing its presence problematizes some of the chief assumptions made about doing feminist empowerment research: that we can eliminate power from our interactions, that researchers can be fully transparent in motive and location.

For example, I felt that in order to gain access to collective workers I would have to de-emphasize the academic aspect of my interest in the project. Academics are often viewed by activists as 'ivory tower elitists' who know little about the real lives of women; conversely, academics often view activists as lacking knowledge and their work as inadequately informed by theory. Part of my role as a feminist researcher has been to juggle my multiple locations so as to gain access. This is not to say that I lied or deceived the women in my sample; however, I de-emphasized my academic credentials and instead stressed my experience working within collectives. I also shared some of my views on the work that I saw them doing, and stated my desire to work for organizational democracy by bringing forward and documenting their experiences. The tension I experienced between my roles as academic and activist reflects the tensions we often confront within our own subjectivities and locations, not only when conducting research, but more generally in our lives where it is quite common to feel uncomfortable gaps between our own feelings and intentions, on the one hand, and how we are perceived, on the other. Valerie Walkerdine (1990) has described similar tensions in her role as an observer of a working-class British family, noting that one element of the relationship between researcher and researched is the experience of being different from each other and at the same time wanting to be similar. According to Walkerdine, this almost paradoxical insider–outsider location should not be disavowed or denied, but recognized as a usual part of the relationship dynamic between researcher and participants in community research. Such dynamics bear watching where pragmatic advantage (such as getting access to collectives, in my case) hangs in the balance between personal subjectivities and public presentation.

At the time of the feminist collectives project I did not fully appreciate the complexities of power relations in the research process, and felt that in de-emphasizing my role as academic and valuing their role as activists I was effectively relinquishing the power that is often given academics who are viewed as 'experts'. In truth, of course, the very fact that I was doing the research put me in a position of power. Some collectives came to see me as an 'expert' on organizational issues; one woman humorously referred to me as the 'collective doctor'.

An additional, converse power play here is that through doing this research I did become 'knowing': Often I saw dynamics within collectives or between workers that I wanted to comment on, but the activist in me felt the academic had no business doing so, while the academic worried that playing 'collective doctor' would jeopardize the research process. I had questions about my responsibilities and my role. Thus in some instances I avoided giving advice I had confidence in, for fear that it could only produce a 'power-over' relationship, while at other times I took advantage of the expert role to advance my own research.

In reflecting on this process, what has become clear to me is the affective dimension that arises both from the web of power relations between the researcher and the researched and from the contradictions we each experience within our own subjectivities (see also Morgen, 1983). For all our attacks on positivism and 'objectivity', feminist researchers too have denied some of the feelings that affect the interaction, reporting, and outcomes of community research projects.

Both power and responsibility are inherent in the role of a researcher who comes into a situation and stirs up issues by asking questions; who demands reflection and analysis from research participants; and who terminates the project when she has her data regardless of the far-reaching implications that the project may have for the participants. At the same time, the research participants may exercise their power and either refuse to continue with the research or insist on exploring only certain kinds of questions and issues. In this 'knowledge/power couplet', the relationship between researcher and participants is complex and reciprocal. To deny these power relations and their effect on the research is to obscure further the already complex and often contradictory research process (see also Harding, 1987). Not acknowledging the researcher's power as 'discoverer' can be as disabling and patronizing for research participants as overestimating that power.

My initial reflections on this process have stressed my locations as an academic and an activist, a former collective worker and a current researcher, and have brought forward the tensions and the emotional aspect of the power relations that operate in community research. But they have glossed over the relevance of my social identity as a lesbian and its effect on the research process. Power is inevitably implicated in social identities when some are privileged over others.

Further Reflections

In my research with feminist social-service collectives I was very interested in eliminating heterosexist (as well as sexist and racist) bias: even though this was not a 'lesbian topic', the questions I wanted to ask, and in fact one of the primary motivations for undertaking the project, came from my experiences as a lesbian worker in collectives. Yet in the methodology section of my report I did not reveal my lesbian identity, although I did comment on the many other locations and identities that had informed my work. Thus I did not completely adhere to feminist research principles on the criterion of transparency: I did not reveal everything that informed my analysis; I was not completely honest with the reader; and I was not honest with myself. This is not an apology. I was quite sensibly worried about the implications of revealing myself in print as lesbian: would the dissertation be accepted? would I get a job? and so on. (Now more out lesbians do get their work published, but not in every field, and often their work is viewed as offering a narrow perspective.) At times I succeeded in convincing myself that my lesbian identity had nothing significant to do with my research or analysis. I did look at race, class, and sexuality as issues within collectives and wrote about these. Thus I had done the 'right kind' of feminist analysis. But I did not make the links between my identity as a lesbian and the theoretical framework, research questions, and methodology of the research project. Now that I have a secure job and work openly on lesbian topics, many of these conflicts have eased. But the principle of starting from the personal, common to current guidelines for feminist research, can in fact be experienced by lesbian researchers as heterosexist. Feminist principles require that we be honest in the research process without recognizing the privilege inherent in this demand. Frank self-identification is perhaps merely good, accountable practice for white, heterosexual women; but for other, marginalized identities it often poses a risk of grave professional damage, and to make it a research requirement for lesbians is tantamount to 'outing'. To be able to acknowledge fully the ways in which 'fragmented identities' shape our work is a rare privilege when one of those identities is lesbian. Moreover, identifying oneself as lesbian can misrepresent the research if readers essentialize that identity or see it as reducing the research to a narrow scope. Foucault, for example, rarely identified himself as gay in print, for similar reasons; yet clearly his location affected the questions he was able to ask about the history of sexuality. At the same time, researchers who set aside the principle of public self-disclosure still need to reflect on the power plays attendant on their undisclosed identities. I will describe many of these power issues in the next section, on my research on lesbian abuse.

Methodological Issues In Research On Lesbian Topics

In my current research on abuse in lesbian relationships, I am 'out' and feel better about the integrity of this work because I can clearly indicate how it is informed by my experiences as a lesbian, but many power issues remain. This research in particular raises questions about my responsibilities to lesbian communities when writing about some of the more negative aspects of lesbian lives.

Such research is sensitive because of the reactions within heterosexist universities that continue to see work on gay and lesbian issues as narrow in focus or lacking scientific merit. Claire Renzetti, a heterosexual who has done the most comprehensive research in this area to date, describes the reactions that she received from within the university. She writes about these in the preface of her book *Violent betrayal: Partner abuse in lesbian relationships* (1992: 3):

> . . . I was unprepared for a number of my colleagues' reactions to this particular project. Some implied that my reputation might be sullied; after all, why would anyone who is not a lesbian care about problems in lesbian relationships? Others expressed an interest in a voyeuristic sort of way; they apparently classified lesbians and lesbian relationships as 'exotic'. Still others regarded the research as silly; in their opinion, lesbian battering was not a topic worthy of scientific study.

Renzetti's experiences and the debates within lesbian and feminist communities illustrate some of the difficulties faced by researchers working in areas that are defined by the identities of marginalized social groups—women, lesbians, blacks—and are therefore 'sensitive': in other words, inherently political.

Much of the published research in the area of lesbian abuse is quantitative and parallels the positivist research designs that have often been used in research on heterosexual abuse. There seems to have been a desire to legitimize research in this area by following non-feminist, heterosexist paradigms, leaving all the assumptions of previous works unchallenged, and paying little attention to feminist methodological approaches or critiques (Brown, 1989; Lenskyj, 1990). What is striking is the absence of any reflexive analysis of the researchers' locations: that is, examination of the subjectivities that researchers bring to their work or analysis of what Edward Said (1989) calls the 'strategic formation' of research—the self-perpetuating system of referential power in the field within which we think and work (Said, 1989; Opie, 1992) that leaves authoritative works in place, whatever their limitations.

My own independent research project (separate from my work with CLOSE) in the area of abuse in lesbian relationships involves several components: a survey of lesbian communities to uncover the prevalence of abuse and the forms that it takes; in-depth interviews with lesbians to learn about their experiences within relationships, patterns of abuse, relationship dynamics, experiences when seeking and receiving help, and constructions of this form of abuse; and corresponding interviews with service providers and counsellors on their constructions of it. Working within a feminist postmodernist framework, I want to bring forward lesbians' voices and analyze the social discourses available to lesbians that give meaning to their experiences (Gavey, 1989). I am also examining the larger institutional and community contexts that shape the responses to abuse in lesbian relationships.

In the course of this work many methodological issues have arisen that point to the need for reflexive analysis when reporting on research. I will provide an overview of some of these issues by discussing my own experiences in obtaining funding, recruiting participants, conducting interviews, and analyzing data. Having focused on the effect of the researcher's identity on achieving transparency in the discussion of power plays in my feminist collective research, I will now highlight some power issues that arise because of the broader social context.

Funding

Not surprisingly, the funding process for most community research has tended to reflect a 'strategic formation' that values quantitative work and a positivist, heterosexist paradigm. (See Chapter 7 for a discussion of recent changes whereby in some cases collaborative partnerships are now encouraged.) I succeeded in obtaining funding for all sections of this research project, but later learned (thanks to a supportive research officer) that there had been much discussion about my application for funds. The reviewers' comments suggested that the subject of abuse in lesbian relationships was too narrow, while others wondered how 25 interviews could be a representative sample, even though I was not claiming that it would be representative. The research officer's advice was to always build into my applications a lengthy section on the merits of qualitative research. Yet underlying her comments I felt there was a message for me, as a lesbian doing lesbian research, that I had better be especially careful to produce an unassailably strong funding application. The comment suggesting that this research area was too narrow hinted at the subtle ways in which funding agencies can exert power through their function as gatekeepers.

Participants

The powerful effects of homophobia and invisibility make it difficult to find participants for any research project of this kind (Herek and Berrill, 1992). Winnipeg is a city of approximately 650,000 people, with one lesbian bar and one gay and lesbian resource centre. I advertised my research in newsletters and through posters at these sites. But finding participants also required innovation because of the sensitivity of the topic. To reach women who might be afraid to be seen tearing off my phone number from a poster, my research assistants and I also placed posters in the cubicles of the bathrooms at the lesbian bar. This was by far the most successful method: many of the women I interviewed mentioned that this allowed them time to read the posters, find out who I was, and take the phone number without being seen; some also said they felt less alone when they saw that other people had taken numbers.

Attracting participants through purposive sampling limits the range of people we are able to reach out to. It also means that the sites of sampling available, in this case primarily the lesbian bar, have to become part of the research as well. The bar was the touchstone, the common element that connected the women I was interviewing, and I needed to include this factor in my written report: that is, how the power effects of social marginalization can limit the research sample.

In addition, some of my assumptions about the most appropriate language to use in recruiting participants were challenged. On the posters and in the survey and interview questions I used the word 'lesbian' exclusively. Yet the first woman I interviewed revealed that she was not sure if she qualified for the research because she was married to a man, involved with a woman, and considered herself to be 'gay', an identity she saw as preferable to the more stigmatized one of 'lesbian'. This encounter pointed to the danger of using rigid identity categories, as well as the effects of language.

Interviews

In general, feminist ethical guidelines for research acknowledge the power of the researcher and aim to protect participants from its misuse. But researchers too are subject to power dynamics that can affect the course of research. Many ethical issues arose in the process of arranging and conducting the interviews, among them safety. Initially I was most concerned with the emotional safety of the participants, wanting to offer them a place where they would feel comfortable. Once, though, when I went to a woman's home to do an interview, she revealed that her violent partner was out of jail; I could feel myself tense and rush through the interview for fear that her ex-lover would barge in and become violent. At this and other moments I was very aware of my own safety issues. For instance, I was never sure who was calling to be interviewed—a perpetrator, a survivor, someone who happened to get my phone number? In part for safety's sake, most of the interviews were conducted in my office at the University of Manitoba and others at the more centrally located University of Winnipeg. But this was not an ideal arrangement. Many of the participants were unfamiliar with either university and found it intimidating to go there. The power of abusers to intimidate permeated the interview process, leading me to make changes that set off other power effects.

Ethical issues centred on the need to ensure confidentiality and anonymity. Lesbian communities are relatively small; I knew some of the women who came for interviews and knew of or had seen before many others. We had to talk at length about how we would react if we ran into each other in public. I also began to hear about some batterers who had been in relationships with several women. Learning that someone was currently being verbally abused by a woman who, I knew from other interviews, had a history of escalating domestic violence raised questions about my ethical responsibilities. Generally, I followed the same guidelines that therapists follow. I would not disclose to a woman that I had already heard about her abusive partner, because that would have violated someone else's confidentiality.

But tensions often arose between my role as interviewer and the temptation to take on the power of the counsellor's role. This was a fine line to walk. Women were telling me stories that many had never told anyone before. They were generous with the information they provided, allowing me to read personal letters, look at photographs, and listen to tape-recorded telephone conversations; many came with bags of letters and other 'evidence'. I offered them a resource booklet on abuse in lesbian relationships and a list of services, books, and names of counsellors that I thought could provide supportive counselling. I also let them know that I would keep them informed about the progress of the research and that they could call me if they had questions, concerns, or more information. Once, however, I did slip into a counselling mode. The woman in question was the perpetrator of violence in her relationship, and disclosed that she was currently both emotionally and physically violent. In this instance, feeling that there was a grey area to my ethical responsibilities, I made the decision to try to affect her behaviour, even though as a research participant she would reasonably have expected simply to provide me with information. I tried to talk with her about ways of avoiding abusive behaviour, and encouraged her to seek help.

Listening to the tapes of the interviews afterwards, I could hear myself struggling to avoid slipping into a counselling mode. I was aware of my own resistance to taking in the painful memories that were shared with me. My 'uh huhs' and 'okays' at times sounded detached—as if I were passing judgement, when that was not what I had intended. My own feelings, then, affected my conduct as interviewer and consequently, perhaps, the course of the interview.

Data analysis

Immediately following each interview, I recorded my reflections about it on tape, including the themes that stood out, the tone, the body language, and my reactions and responses.

I also discussed the taped interviews with the three research assistants who were transcribing them. I would ask them for feedback both on my own role as interviewer and on the content of the interview. Since these assistants, though all lesbians, were otherwise diverse in their social locations, consulting with them provided a useful check on the power effects of my own responses as a white, now middle-class lesbian. It also helped to maintain confidentiality, since we talked to each other and did not have to de-brief with others who were not connected to the research. Finally, this process brought forward our various locations and subjectivities and made me more aware of the emotional responses and attitudes that battered lesbians encounter. The assistants' reactions—such as 'Why doesn't she leave?', 'This is only one side of the story', or 'Is this really abuse?'—underlined the sensitivity of this topic not only for heterosexual researchers like Renzetti (1992), but for lesbians as well.

Conclusions

Articulating a reflexive analysis and exploring our own subjectivities and locations as researchers are necessary in order to bring forward questions of accountability such as 'Why am I doing this research?' and 'Who am I doing it for?' What I can conclude is that feminist researchers are correct in noting that our identities, locations, and experiences do shape our work. My history as a lesbian will inevitably inform my research (just as a straight woman's will inform hers) even when it does not seem central to the topic, and even if I cannot be open about how it informs my work. Thus I agree with the feminist research ideal according to which we must acknowledge the multiple identities and locations we bring to our work. Because lesbian identity is both stigmatized and invisible, however, there is not only motivation to conceal it but opportunity as well. Exercising the choice to announce a lesbian sexual orientation in a homophobic culture makes adherence to feminist research guidelines far riskier for us than for heterosexual women.

That said, it is also important to consider what we are revealing when naming our sexual identity in the research process. Judith Butler (1991: 15) raises the provocative question 'Can sexuality even remain sexuality when it submits to a criterion of transparency and disclosure?' In other words, what does naming myself as a lesbian reveal? Butler's work points to the ways in which assumptions are derived from viewing the category 'lesbian' that then serve to specify one's identity in ways that support rather than dismantle the categories of heterosexist and homophobic thought. For example, you may read my research as an example of 'lesbian work' and claim to now understand what it means to be a lesbian, thereby keeping the category of heterosexuality in place, as the norm. This is clearly not my intention; therefore it is important to read the examples that I have described as reflecting not an inner truth, but a social performance—an enactment or reinvention—of the category 'lesbian'. Exploring the negotiations involved in the performance of our identities in our research projects is one way of seeing how power operates.

Our feminist research process will begin to achieve the ideals of starting from the personal, stating our assumptions, and striving for integrity when we fully acknowledge all the power relations at play in social research. As Kitzinger (1991) reminds us, 'power and knowledge . . . are inextricably connected'. As feminists we discover this when we study the social construction of knowledge. What we cannot forget is that as researchers we too are constructing knowledge. Writing about power as it operates in the research process is necessary to keep our work honest.

My intention in this chapter has been primarily to explore the power issues that arise in the research process through examination of the situations that have arisen in my research projects on feminist collectives and lesbian abuse. Many of these experiences, though personal, are relevant to the power issues that arise not only in other forms of community research but with respect to other identities, such as race, class, and gender. The guidelines that I use in my own research are reprinted in Appendix III. Since many of the power plays discussed here stemmed from my identity as a lesbian or my lesbian research topic, some of these guidelines may not be transferable to other research, but others are general enough to apply to power issues not specific to lesbians, and can be developed for other locations, identities, and topics.

6

Creative Analyses

> We were pushed to develop our analysis further by the women in the study. . . . They were hesitant about being negative, but were clearly critical. . . . They wanted us the researchers to interpret their experience to them (Acker, Barry, and Esseveld, 1983: 429).

Advancing emancipatory goals without dictating to women how they should see their lives has been a long-standing conundrum for feminists. This was of central concern for Acker, Barry, and Esseveld (1983: 429-30) as they struggled between "'letting [the middle-aged women in their study] talk for themselves" and put[ting] those experiences into . . . a framework that links women's oppression to the structure of Western capitalist society'. The women themselves wanted more than a mirroring of their own interpretations; they hoped that these feminist academics would help them to make sense of the uncertainties, ambiguities, and transitions they faced in their efforts to move from the mother/wife role into the paid labour market. This demand, the researchers found, could not be met by joining with the interviewed women in developing a critical analysis. Not only was such an approach impractical in many instances, but they felt that in order to work collaboratively with the women they would have to confine their research to women ideologically similar to themselves. Although in this way they would avoid imposing their own world view on the research participants, such an approach would also contravene their political and research aspirations to understand women's diverse and changing situations and how these affect women's consciousness. Reluctantly, they concluded that as social scientists they were responsible for reconstructing social reality in a way that looked beyond people's immediate understandings to less apparent patterns of social relations.

Research as empowerment does not resolve the conundrum of the 'power plays' that are inextricable from any research act. Instead, it deliberately increases the complexity of the research process by employing an analytical approach that doubles back on itself. In part, this doubling-back is accomplished by the transparency and reflexivity demonstrated by Acker, Barry, and Esseveld in their honest (and courageous) portrayal of the contradictions between their political beliefs and their analytical practices. Likewise in this chapter, I use self-reflexivity to highlight the tension between giving voice to women's experiences and analyzing these voices. My approach differs, however, in taking a postmodern tack. Whereas Acker, Barry, and Esseveld undertook a dialectical analysis of the interaction between societal structures and individual consciousness to reconstruct reality, I intentionally juxtapose mutually contradictory methods of analysis in order to keep the interpretations unsettled and open to question.

My purpose is twofold: to make sense of the information gained in the research process without imposing definitive conclusions, and to support confident action without dictating the course to be followed. In both cases, the point is to counter the dogmatism that tends to accompany assertions, whether of interpretation or of recommendations, and undermines even the best efforts to challenge violent control and establish democratic relations. These processes and their products, which I call 'creative analyses', generate the 'links and interruptions' central to research as empowerment and lead to the formulation of 'alternative truths' and the creation of 'inclusive communities'.

PRINCIPLED CREATIVITY

> **Creative analyses:** thinking outside the confines of dominant assumptions and the researcher's own interpretations, to invent alternative truths.

Creative analyses are means of reconsidering power and its use by generating alternatives to dominant assumptions about social relations. Whereas traditional data analysis is seen as part of an objective process of positivist research that builds on existing knowledge, in research as empowerment we recognize the constructedness of all analyses, and the importance of challenging not only widely held beliefs but the researcher's own perspectives on the subject in question. Developing creative analyses means listening for the competing discourses, distinguishing how each one seeks to construct social relations in line with its own view of reality and political interests (see Parker, 1992), and then deconstructing these discourses by baring their implicit assumptions and undermining their logic (see Culler, 1982), in order to disrupt those assumptions and make possible an ongoing redevelopment of political positions. There are and can be no set ways of going about this kind of analysis; rather, a series of dilemmas must be repeatedly negotiated (Burman and Parker, 1993).

In my own research, I pursue creative analyses by moving back and forth among my own evolving theories, the findings from the study in question, and my anticipations of the audiences for whom I am preparing my interpretations. Throughout these fluctuations, I am guided and sustained by the understandings developed through feminist dialogue and working with others for social change, which help me to keep the aims of empowerment in the foreground. While the interpretative processes and conclusions shift, I work to build 'inclusive communities' by following four principles:

1. expanding dichotomies;
2. speaking with those about whom I am speaking;
3. appreciating discourses; and
4. displacing logics.

The first principle advances a critical analysis of power by increasing the range of possible constructions of reality and thus disrupting the usual binary ('either/or') oppositions; this helps to 'bridge the gaps' between people from different positions. The second principle fosters a responsible use of power by keeping the study 'grounded' in the subjectivities of the people in question. The third principle helps to make sense of a range of positions while making their respective holders feel appreciated as well as encouraged to expand their understanding. The fourth principle is a reminder that each position has a respectable logic that can be turned back on itself to spin power relations off balance and towards a new balance. Together, these four principles not only maintain the analyst's links with the research participants and, more broadly, with movements for social change, but ensure that as successive modes of interpretation, consistent with each principle, are adopted, earlier conclusions are disrupted.

These principles helped me to analyze a wide range of emotionally laden, irreconcilable positions on the unionization of shelters for abused women and their children. This chapter outlines the theoretically incompatible methods of analysis that I combined in order to interpret one particularly controversial area of the study, the effect of unionization on interactions between shelter workers and managers.[1] This approach, which, as we shall see, is not without precedent, helped to loosen my views, and possibly others', on the labour unionization of women. The particular combination of methods used in this case reflects my gravitation towards approaches for which I felt an affinity as a feminist. I selected approaches that would be useful for identifying a range of women's perspectives (from both labour and management), for making sense of these perspectives so they each could be understood and as a group could be acted upon, and for displacing these perspectives so that social activists would not become fixed on any one conclusion or solution.

In carrying out the analysis I drew on various qualitative streams of research and borrowed extensively from the methods proposed by several male theorists. Such borrowing has been criticized by some feminists as generating dependencies that sap, distort, or derail feminist thinking and action. Countering this tendency to unquestioningly reject postmodern methods, the Canadian feminist Kathleen Martindale (1994: 110) writes: 'Instead of focusing on the question of whether deconstruction compromises the ethical certainty of demands underlying feminist criticism, the debate has centred on whether or not feminist critics should use "male" theory'. In my view, links with feminist activists in shelters, other women's programs, and academic circles made it possible for me to borrow what I saw as helpful from various male qualitative researchers and to reframe their insights and strategies within a principled approach to the analysis and use of power. Moreover, the specific area of this study—the unionization of shelters for abused women and their children—ensured that their methods were tested and reformulated within the context of women's struggles for a better life.

UNIONIZATION AND UNITY

Like many other feminists in the 1980s, I hoped that within the shelter movement we could formulate a coherent philosophy to guide us in achieving 'unity among women'. For this very purpose I struggled to redraft the statement of philosophy of the shelter that I had worked to establish (Pennell, 1987), and returned to the United States with the intent of doing doctoral research on shelter structures. Learning that staff at one local shelter had joined a labour union, I wondered what effect 'unionization' might have on the hoped-for 'union' among women. Would it split women along class lines (labour/management), or would it draw women together in co-governing their organizations?

In 1986 and 1987, while pursuing my doctoral studies, I undertook a first round of interviews with labour and management at unionized shelters across Canada and the United States. By telephone and, less frequently, in person, I asked questions about the reasons for unionizing, the process itself, and its effects. According to various accounts, the workers had joined the unions partly to enrich their meagre pay and benefit packages, but above all to resolve personnel and philosophical conflicts resulting from increases in staff size, role specialization, and hierarchical organization. For some shelters, negotiating the first collective agreement made relations between workers and management even worse; but for a sizeable number, bargaining brought the two sides closer together. Interested in finding solutions, I focused on the latter examples and identified a process that I called 'consensual bargaining' (Pennell, 1990a). Such bargaining, I learned, made it possible for labour and management to bring out their divergent interests at the table (not a simple matter in these small, closely knit, mission-oriented organizations), while the necessity of reaching a consensus pushed each side to listen to the other's views more carefully than they otherwise might have, and to integrate these into agreements that all could uphold. When I began teaching at the University of Manitoba, I heard more about labour–management conflicts both at white shelters and, increasingly, in aboriginal programs. I then carried out a more comprehensive second round of interviews with labour and management at shelters organized before or during 1989. By this time I was hoping to initiate a co-operative endeavour between the Canadian and US shelter movements that would facilitate self-study and collective action. The response from domestic-violence coalitions and unionized shelters was overwhelmingly supportive. Every shelter association in Canada and the United States was willing to help me find local unionized shelters. And every identified unionized shelter (22 in Canada, 8 in the US) responded to the request to interview members about their experience of labour organization. In lengthy interviews, 32 labour representatives (29 staff in the bargaining unit, three union agents) and 36 management representatives (32 administrators or supervisors outside the bargaining unit and four board representatives, of whom two were men) outlined their experiences of unionization in small women's organizations and speculated on the compatibility of feminism and unionism. Research participants did not simply respond to questions; they recounted, reflected on, and interpreted their own experiences. My primary role was to ensure full, if flexible, coverage of all the areas included in the interview guide, and in addition to summarize key themes and affirm the importance of the respondents' experiences and perspectives. The focus remained on the respondent, while I situated myself as one shelter participant speaking to another. As long as I guaranteed anonymity, they agreed that I would provide each unionized shelter and domestic-violence coalition with a copy of the initial report for them to comment on, and later incorporate their feedback into subsequent publications.

The collaborative ethos appeared intact until I sat down to analyze the interview transcripts alone in my study, at a physical and psychological distance from the interviewees. In preparing the initial report to mail back to the shelters and associations, I struggled with the problem of how to retain my original emphasis on collaborative action. As Acker, Barry, and Esseveld found in their study, the problem did not go away. I identified with the shelter participants and admired their commitment both to ending violence against women and children and to creating non-abusive workplaces. While recognizing the limits of merely affirmative work, I wanted to present them with a document in which they and I could identify our voices with pride and view our differences as a basis for mutual learning and co-operative planning. However, I recognized that research undertaken according to feminist ethical principles may mean naming differences (of race, sexual identity, class, etc.) that might be unsettling for some participants.

The difficulty of adhering to these principles emerged starkly as I sought to interpret the participants' statements on the very sensitive topic of labour–management interactions. All but four of the 68 participants had offered their views on this subject, many holding forth at length without any prompting on my part. They spoke with intensity of the effects that unionization had, for better or worse, on how administrators and board directors reached decisions with or about staff, and how management and labour related to each other. In listening, I was repeatedly struck by the wide divergence in views both within and between shelters. As interviewer, I knew that I needed to avoid taking sides, to attend respectfully to all participants' views and to help them elaborate on the reasons behind their positions. Yet as interpreter I had to make sense of the disjunctions; no longer focusing on each research participant as an individual, I found myself wavering between relativistic acceptance of all views and judgemental ranking on their individual merits.

After retracing my steps a number of times, I eventually arrived at an analytical strategy that, at least for now, meets what I see as the demands of creative analyses. The result, however, was not the collaborative effort for which I had hoped. Rather, I worked alone to analyze the information, moving between identifying the interviewees' positions (which I came to refer to as 'images') and making sense of and then disrupting their projections of labour–management interactions until I could present a summary that answered my original question about how unionization affected their relationships. What follows is an account of the steps I took to analyze the information I had gathered. The following outline of analytical strategies is not meant to be prescriptive, but to show how different approaches can be combined when following the principles of 'creative analyses': expanding dichotomies, speaking with those about whom we are speaking, appreciating discourses, and displacing logics. Through this principled strategy I demonstrate how 'feminist links' can be built while interrupting habitual ways of thinking.

Principle 1: Expanding Dichotomies

For much of the interview material I could readily apply quantitative modes of summarizing and analyzing. Using content analysis (Krippendorff, 1980), I reduced statements to thematic units to be counted and ranked, and tested the significance of relationships among variables. For instance, I placed on a scale ('better' to 'unchanged' to 'worse') reports of the impact of unionization on pay rates and benefit packages. But this approach was far too binding to deal with the variety and complexity of the statements on labour–management interactions. I was also concerned that such a presentation would aggravate the tendency within the shelter movement either to champion unionization or to condemn it. Wanting to promote constructive dialogue, I turned to my first principle for creative analyses, expanding dichotomies. Carrying out this analyses, however, was in no way straightforward.

From the beginning I encountered a dilemma based in the 'either/or' nature of categorization: to claim that an interviewee's statement fits one image of unionization is to assert that it does not fit another. This dilemma was heightened by the political aims of the study, which pushed me to define the boundaries around each image, so that participants could differentiate between their own and others' perspectives and use this comparison for purposes of dialogue and joint planning. Knowing from experience that 'black and white' distinctions are rarely accurate and often conceal imperialistic motives, I attempted to generate less polarized images. To this end, I employed first the semiotic square proposed by Algirdas J. Greimas, which provided a starting-point but in the end proved inadequate on its own, and later Barney Glaser and Anselm Strauss's constant comparative method, which grounded the images in the respondents' own statements. Together, these analytic tools enabled me to take a systematic approach to discerning various perspectives and placing them within a global vision of the network of images. This approach allowed me not to 'escape' dichotomies—an impossibility in a system based on categories—but instead to expand the dichotomies within my conceptual field.

The Semiotic Square

Dichotomies can be expanded by generating a **semiotic square** consisting of the four reciprocal positions within a discourse:

(1) a key starting position	(2) its contrary
(4) its implication (neither 1 nor 2)	(3) its contradiction (both 1 and 2)

One effective way of moving beyond binary oppositions and forming a fuller set of interconnected categories is to work from Greimas's (1983) semiotic square. This model (which builds on the work of the Swiss structural linguist Ferdinand de Saussure) recognizes that meaning lies in the difference between concepts: an idea is rendered meaningful not by its reference to a certain reality but by its placement within a linguistic arrangement or structure whose parts give each other meaning (Benveniste, 1971). The four-cornered square is generated by making all possible logical combinations of the opposition between two concepts. As Schleifer (1987) points out, the square includes an either/or opposition (the contrary) as well as a both/and relationship (the contradiction) and a neither/nor negation (the implication). At the same time, the square meets Greimas's (1990) analytical criteria of internal coherence, exhaustiveness of all possibilities, and simplicity. The semiotic square moves us beyond opposition to resolution by directing us to comprehend meaning in a holistic manner (Jameson, 1972).

A False Start

I started my analysis with Greimas's square in the hope that it would offer an overall picture within which I could distinguish various perspectives on unionization and at the same time bring them together. After reviewing the interview transcripts, I constructed a square that identified four basic positions according to their awareness of class divisions. Although I portrayed the set of positions in a square, I ranked them in my mind from least to most desirable, with a linear progression from false consciousness to class consciousness. At the lowest level of this progression was the starting point, Cell 1, *concealing* class divisions and hence rejecting unionization as intrusive and divisive. Cell 2, the contrary of Cell 1, is the highest level of class consciousness, in which class divisions were revealed (as in acknowledged), and the contract was seen as *removing* those divisions by confirming in law the shelter's collective structure. Between these extremes, Cell 3 contained the second-highest level of consciousness, the contradiction; in this view, class divisions were both concealed and revealed through 'consensual bargaining', which highlighted employee–employer differences while promoting mutually acceptable resolutions; unionization became a means of *redrawing* organizational lines so that management and labour could become partners in the struggle to gain more leverage in negotiations with the funding body. Finally, in Cell 4, the implication represented the second-lowest level of consciousness, in which class divisions were neither concealed nor revealed; here the contract served to lessen unfair labour practices without acknowledging its role in *reinforcing* managerial control.

While this model met Greimas's analytical criterion of internal coherency, it was essentially speculative, not empirical, and I quickly rejected it on two specific counts. First, even a cursory rereading of the data did not support some of the categories: in particular, the comments that I had judged to be 'concealing' were not denying class divisions but articulating interviewees' experiences, what they had learned through participating in unionized shelters. Second, far from fostering dialogue, the categories would only increase tensions among shelter participants. This false start heightened my awareness of the different tracks down which interpretation can proceed, the influence of my biases, and the necessity of remaining linked with the interviewees, especially when working alone in my study. It did not lead me to abandon Greimas's semantic strategy, however; I still wanted to generate multiple angles on unionization within a square showing how they fitted together.

When my first attempt at diagramming perspectives on organized shelters fell short, I took some consolation in Fredric Jameson's words in his foreword to Greimas's *On Meaning:* the square offers a 'visual device to map out and articulate a set of relationships that it is much more confusing, and much less economical, to convey in expository prose. . . . however, experience testifies that you must blacken many pages before you get it right' (1987: xv).

PRINCIPLE 2: SPEAKING WITH

Speaking with: creating categories based on what research participants actually say. It entails seven steps:

    (1) listening closely to what the research participants are saying;

    (2) comparing their statements;

    (3) noticing interesting or recurring themes;

    (4) giving a name to each theme (categorizing it);

    (5) checking each category against more statements;

    (6) clarifying each category against the other categories being developed; and

    (7) reshaping the categories to fit participants' statements.

If I was to expand dichotomies in a constructive manner, I needed to continue listening to the shelter participants and to imagine their readings of my analyses. In other words, I required a mode of analysis that followed my second principle, 'speaking with' the interviewees. I turned to Glaser and

Strauss's constant comparative method in order to reformulate my original square by basing its four positions on what the shelter participants themselves had conveyed to me. In part, this strategy could be characterized as analytical induction (see Denzin, 1989; Hyde, 1994) in that I moved back and forth between deduction, in which I tested my tentative square against the interviewees' statements, and induction, in which I reshaped the categories on the basis of their statements. By working from the square's four corners, I did not narrow in on one hypothesis with universal applicability, but rather filled out a robust set of competing hypotheses.

The Constant Comparative Method

The constant comparative method proceeds by placing together various statements having some interesting commonality and gradually developing a category for analysis. A category is refined by including further items or by comparing it with other categories being developed. Glaser and Strauss (1967: 61) stop adding items when a category is 'saturated': that is, when further data no longer enhance theoretical understanding of the concept (see also Kirby and McKenna, 1989; Strauss and Corbin, 1990). In the shelter study, however, I continued adding more items in order to determine the number of interviewees expressing a certain view. This made it possible to determine which views were the more prevalent.

Glaser and Strauss see their methodology as inducing categories directly from the data and from this empirical foundation discovering 'grounded theory'. Their intent is not to test pre-set hypotheses against data but rather to 'validate' theory: to develop, check, and refine the evolving theory with reference to the data (Strauss and Corbin, 1990: 138); they are 'equivocal' on whether the emerging hypotheses are confirmed by the data (Hammersley, 1989: 198). An assertion that the theory is confirmed becomes problematic when it is recognized that the researcher does not merely discover it from the data but also shapes this 'discovery'. Glaser and Strauss acknowledge that researchers' capacity to generate insightful theories (their 'theoretical sensitivity') is influenced by their personalities and experiences as well as their previously developed 'categories and hypotheses'. Nevertheless, they intentionally emphasize the emergence of plausible, relevant, and meaningful ideas out of the data (Glaser and Strauss, 1967: 46). In my unionization study, Glaser and Strauss's theory of knowledge was helpful in redirecting my interpretations back to the voices of the participants. Used on its own, however, without the semiotic square, it would have obscured the pre-existing assumptions that initially led me to target certain views for criticism.

Although my false start had revealed how prejudices can skew theoretical sensitivity, it also showed the utility of the square in setting out my analytical presuppositions. My second effort to specify the shelter participants' positions worked back and forth between constructing a square and attending to their words. The provisional series of squares compelled me to identify the concept under scrutiny and the point from which the analysis commenced. As Fredric Jameson stresses, where we begin is 'actively determinant in astonishing ways' of where we end (Greimas, 1987: xv).

Four Images

In rereading closely the interviewees' comments, I returned to my original reason for undertaking this study: to find out whether unionization split shelter participants into labour and management sides or, as I hoped, could overcome class divisions and thus contribute to unity among women. My starting-point was no longer the negative finding of 'false consciousness' ('concealing') but instead the wish that women could be united. I used the semiotic square to prepare tentative diagrams of its four categories or 'images' of experience. The constant comparative method helped me to refine these images and eventually to name them, as follows (for a fuller discussion, see Pennell, 1995):

Unites (unionization unites). The first image, in cell 1, was less a reality than a hope that labour unionization could bring women together into one body and overcome the societal pressures dividing them into labour and management (the earlier 'removing'). This image was presented by a single interviewee who described labour and management as covertly joining forces against the government representative supposedly bargaining on behalf of the board of directors. While rare as a description of actual practice, this image was significant because it reflected the expressed aspirations of a number of the interviewees.

Alienates (unionization divides). In cell 2, across from 'unites', was its contrary, 'alienates': the idea that unionization divides or estranges labour and management from each other. This view of the effect of unionization, which I had earlier called 'concealing', was the second most common one, expressed by 24 of the 68 interviewees.

Moderates (unionization both unites and divides). In cell 3, kitty corner from 'unites', was the contradictory 'moderates' (earlier labelled 'reinforcing'). From this angle, unionization in part divides and in part unites labour and management so as to overcome favouritism and ensure fair treatment of each side by the other. Projected by 45 of the shelter participants, this was the most common image of unionization.

Allies (unionization neither divides nor unites). Directly beneath 'unites', in cell 4, was the implication 'allies'. From this perspective, the union neither unites nor divides labour and management (the earlier 'redrawing' position) but links them as partners. According to 15 of the respondents, unionization facilitated exchanges in which employers and employees could advance their separate interests while upholding the common good of all participants.

PRINCIPLE 3: APPRECIATING DISCOURSES

Appreciating discourses: recognizing the merits of various positions within their own layers of context by

(1) sketching an initial picture of the meaning of each position;

(2) checking this guess against different parts of the position;

(3) discerning each position's relevant contexts, both material and philosophical;

(4) mediating among alternative meanings for each position by making sense of it within its various contexts; and

(5) proposing a conceptual framework in which all the different positions increase understanding.

Once these images had been mapped, the next step was to develop an analysis that went beyond delineating positions to promoting mutual understanding: in other words, to seeing each position as one among (possibly) many sensible positions. To accomplish this aim, I turned to my third principle for creative analyses, 'appreciating discourses'. The aim here was to assist shelter participants and others in understanding how each image made sense within the milieu in which it was formed. To this end, I set aside the Glaser–Strauss method, according to which I had removed interviewees' statements from their contexts in order to compare them, and turned to hermeneutic interpretation, in which understanding is achieved through viewing a phenomenon as a whole within its layers of context.

Hermeneutics

Hermeneutics emerged from such traditions as biblical exegesis and Greco-Latin philology and has been developed by a series of theorists in such areas as literary criticism, humanist social science, and critical theory (Ricoeur, 1981). My approach to hermeneutics is heavily indebted to the cultural anthropologist Clifford Geertz's epistemology of 'local knowledge' and to the phenomenological philosopher Paul Ricoeur's ontology of 'proposed worlds', which together led me to search out how people within particular locales envision reality.

Geertz's (1983: 6) aim is 'to turn from trying to explain social phenomena by weaving them into grand textures of cause and effect to trying to explain them by placing them in local frames of awareness'. To comprehend another culture or world view—that is, to gain 'the understanding of understandings' (Geertz, 1983: 5)—the key is not to develop some universal theory or to imagine that one inhabits that culture or holds that world view, but to appreciate the coherency or logic of its discourses from the inside rather than the outside. Geertz (1984) explains that the aim of cultural hermeneutics is to extend oneself to view each logic within its own context as opposed to judging its deviance from the vantage point of foundational claims about the human mind or human nature. To understand another's discourse is not simply an act of appropriating what is alien; as Ricoeur (1981: 162) puts it, 'to interpret is to follow the path of thought opened up by the text, to place oneself en route towards the orient of the text' or its direction of meaning. To recover meaning, Ricoeur (1981: 161) proposes a 'hermeneutical arc' reaching from linguistic structuralism, which uncovers the internal relations of the text, to hermeneutical interpretation, which unfolds the external references that the text is addressing and that give meaning to its contents. This arc focuses the analysis on the text rather than its author's supposed intentions and expands the horizon of understanding by connecting the text with the world to which it refers. The result is to challenge our preconceptions, enlarge our understanding of others, and sharpen our self-reflection.

Contextualizing Feminist Discourses

Paralleling Ricoeur's hermeneutical arc, my unionization study combined the semiotic square (linguistic structuralism) and the constant comparative method (grounded theory) to map the relationships among the positions of the shelter participants, and embarked from this structural analysis to interpret the meanings of these positions. Because each image was a composite of statements from different interviews, I could not rely on any individual speaker's intent to fix its meaning. I could, though, study how the shelter participants' accounts of unionization related to their wider views. By placing the four images, which together covered the full range of perspectives on unionization, in this broader context, I hoped to construct an interpretation consistent with the respondents' beliefs and situations.

Among the recurring points of reference in the interviews were feminist philosophies on how the world is and should be, and, in particular, respondents' view of women's organizations. In all likelihood my introduction to the interviews, in which I referred to unionization as 'an important development in the battered-women's movement', encouraged participants to place their comments within a feminist framework. I suspect, in addition, that my emphasis on sharing the findings in an initial report pushed them to adopt a presumably common language in which to justify their position to their colleagues, both locally and across national boundaries.

In reviewing the transcripts, I found that the respondents did not suggest a single meaning for the term 'feminist'. To sort out its various meanings, I categorized them according to the three most common images of unionization (the fourth image, 'unites', having arisen in only one instance). For those with the 'alienating' image of unionization, adopting a feminist approach meant rejecting a 'heavy-handed' and 'adversarial' 'male model' of interaction, so that women could remain in compassionate alliance. For those with the 'moderating' image it meant creating a 'safety net' and a 'check' system so that women would be adequately compensated and protected. And for those with the 'allying' image it meant achieving a 'legal balancing of power' so that women could make decisions democratically and in both their individual and their mutual interests.

Equally significant, the participants used their feminist beliefs to point out the deficiencies in their respective positions on unionization. Among those who experienced 'alienation', some recognized that the union's masculinist valuation of money enriched staff's economic position in a way that the feminist emphasis on caring had not; among those with the 'moderating' stance, a minority acknowledged that unionization challenged arbitrary rulings by management but hoped that it was only a 'stopgap' on the way to a 'womanist' and 'consensual' organization; and among those with the 'allying' position a number indicated that while unionization fostered consensual bargaining between employers and employees, it failed to establish a system for women as a group to negotiate directly with the real paymaster, the funding body.

The meanings that respondents attributed to the term 'feminist' made eminent sense within their particular settings. 'Alienating' was chiefly projected by people from shelters that had recently unionized, who as a result were gravely concerned about the friction and estrangements exacerbated by the turmoil of the organizing drive and the unfamiliar union processes. Conversely, its contradiction, 'allying', was more common in shelters that, having been organized somewhat longer, had become skilled in friendly collective bargaining. The 'moderating' image had less to do with familiarity with unionization and more to do with the size of the shelter: in shelters with more personnel, collective agreements were seen as a way of clarifying rules and countering unfair practices.

By presenting the logic of each image within 'local frames of awareness', I hoped that my initial report of findings and later publications would promote a greater tolerance of divergent views. By presenting these logics together, I hoped that they would, to use Geertz's (1983: 11) words, 'shed some light on one another'. And I hoped that the good sense of all the images would encourage shelter activists to configure or reconfigure their organizational structures to suit their particular contexts, rather than insist on the correctness of any one approach. In line with these aspirations, I concluded both my initial report (Pennell, 1992) and a later article (Pennell, 1993) with a set of guidelines recommending ways for managers, staff, and union agents to 'fit' bargaining, grievances, and other union processes to the shelter's aims and setting.

The comments that I received on the initial report (which included a feedback sheet) support these hopes: the large majority of the 31 participants who gave an opinion agreed that the initial report of findings presented a 'fair picture of unionized shelters', did not 'leave out a lot of important things that are happening at unionized shelters', and offered helpful guidelines on 'how to approach unionization in a manner that empowers labour and management'. The utility of the study was even more evident in the number of shelters, other women's organizations, and labour unions that requested copies of the reports; the calls from shelters entering into collective negotiations; and the responses at conferences where some attenders said that they had 'snuck' into the presentation because they were afraid of being seen as interested by others from their shelter. Moreover, when I shared strategies gleaned from the study with a local shelter whose workers recently joined a labour union, I found that even though I had undertaken the data analysis on my own, the interactions around the report and its findings renewed the collaborative process with which the project had begun.

Contextualizing discourses made it possible to listen to women's voices and join these voices to a politico-economic analysis. From my perspective, the disunification of women can be attributed to systemic oppression, which feminists can only partially overcome by challenging state control and prefiguring other possibilities within their own organizations (Pennell, 1995). I was able to link the four images to a historical materialist analysis of society without, in my eyes, disrespecting the logic of any one position. For me, this became a solution to the dilemma posed by Acker, Barry, and Esseveld at the outset of this chapter. As interpreter, I was proposing a construction of reality in which women could be unified by appreciating their multiple logics, while as analyst I was at the same time uncovering the structural forces of disunification.

PRINCIPLE 4: DISPLACING LOGICS

In this section I take the analysis one step further, and in a direction that I believe necessary for advancing feminist aims. In all the types of analysis outlined above (linguistic structuralism, grounded theory, and hermeneutics) I drew on the same assumption—and it is politically questionable. Because my starting-point, as reflected in the first cell of my revised square, was a dream

Displacing logics: affirming the incoherence of discourses and thus opening them to alternative viewpoints. It involves	
(1) uncovering the central and assumption of a discourse,	(2) validating its contrary,
(4) upholding the original assumption.	(3) validating its contradiction, while

of unity among women, all four positions in the square represented ways of resolving schisms. Each image implied a solution to estrangement, whether decertifying (in the case of the alienating image) or deploying, reshaping, or transforming collective bargaining (in the three other cases). The irony was that in no case did participants state that they had experienced unification as women, since even the first image, 'unifying', was almost entirely hypothetical (expressed covertly in one solitary instance).

Yet the push for unification was in no way unique to my analysis, and reflected the general philosophy of the shelter movement. A prime example is the 'Principles of Unity' of an American shelter association, the National Coalition Against Domestic Violence (NCADV). When applying to become a member of this coalition and submitting articles to it, I readily assented to NCADV'S requirement that I uphold its stance of inclusivity ('to support and involve battered women of all racial, social, ethnic, religious and economic groups, ages and sexuality') and its political agenda (to 'oppose the use of violence as a means of control over others, and support equality in relationships and the concept of helping women assume power over their own lives'). The NCADV philosophy of unity is further evident in the name of its 1994 national conference, 'Many Voices: One Vision', and its journal, *NCADV Voice*, which has published special issues on eradicating racism (Fall 1989), homophobia (Spring 1991), and classism (Summer 1993) within the shelter movement. While NCADV'S principles are commendable from an empowerment perspective, they also converge with standard criticisms of women in general and feminists in particular. Both within and outside the women's movement, we are repeatedly criticized for disagreeing among ourselves, splintering into factions, and thus undermining our agendas for change. At the same time, we have found that ignoring our differences only creates a false and insupportable sense of homogeneity and consensus (Young, 1990).

To question the 'unification' assumption implicit in my earlier analyses and prevalent in the shelter movement itself, I invoked my fourth principle for creative analysis, displacing logics. My method, in this instance, was based on Jacques Derrida's 'deconstruction', which provided a way of subverting a logic founded on the superiority of union over disunion. Here, in contrast to the case of the semiotic square, the intent is not to define the four interconnected images by means of their differences but instead to overturn the rationality on which the square is founded. The result, as we shall see, is to interrupt set ways of thinking.

Deconstructing the Limits of Women's Unionization

Deconstruction dismantles a philosophy or discourse by stripping it down to its central opposition. Its intent, however, is not to destroy but to borrow a discourse's concepts until its resources have been 'exhausted' and brought to the limit of their utility (1981: 18). The benefit of deconstruction, as Derrida explains, is that in keeping positions 'confounded' (1981: 96), it serves to 'confirm and shake logocentric [rationalistic] and ethnocentric [European-based] assuredness. . . . to transform concepts, to displace them, to turn them against their presuppositions, to reinscribe them in other chains, and little by little to modify the terrain of our work and thereby produce new configurations' (1981: 24).

To this point, my entire analysis—the square, its elaboration in grounded theory, and its contextualization in hermeneutics—rested on, to use Derrida's telling phrase, a 'violent hierarchy' (1981: 41) in which disunion was subordinated to union. In line with the principles of the battered-women's movement, my analysis presupposed that unity is preferable both morally and politically, and that it is a means of ending the violent control of women and children. The square charted a coherent network of the relationships among four images of unionization that were based on women's perspectives and made sense within feminist world views. Yet the analysis, like the statements on which it was based, revealed the limits, the incoherence, of the desire for unity.

As the exercise of displacing logics revealed, the more the participants pushed for solidarity, the more apparent their class divisions as labour and management became, whether in the desire of the 'alienated' to return to a pre-organized state or in the inventive strategies proposed by the advocates of unionization to build more and stronger bridges across their divides. This inversion of disunion over its contrary, union, brought into question the drive to unify women, and displaced, without destroying, the feminist aspiration to bring women together. Thus the result was to assert the necessity of feminist links while disrupting the logic that the union of women is a more worthwhile end than their disunion.

CONCLUSION

This chapter started with the hope that women could advance one another's understanding without getting in the way of the other's development of her own understanding. When the middle-aged women in Acker, Barry, and

Esseveld's study criticized these university researchers, they were pushing them to provide analyses that would extend their own self-knowledge. The researchers wanted to meet this demand but at the same time worried that if they constructed an analysis on their own, rather than collaboratively, they would keep the women from projecting their own voices and understandings. Likewise, in my unionization study, I found it disquieting to carry out an analysis without the ongoing involvement of the shelter participants, especially on a topic provoking so much controversy. To some extent, I resolved this issue by keeping the research oriented to the concerns of the battered-women's movement and by creating opportunities for shelter participants to review my analyses and discuss them with me prior to their wider dissemination.

The source of the wish for a collaborative action methodology was my perception of the necessity for women to take unified action in overcoming violence and instituting democratic relations. The same perception determined the overriding direction of my analysis of the effect of unionization on relations within shelters and channelled me into multiple routes for achieving such solidarity. In order to map these routes, which I have referred to as images, and fit them to the perspectives and contexts of the individuals concerned, I used a series of analytical methods. The further I traced these divergent routes, the more apparent it became that all flowed from the same assumption—the superiority of union over disunion—but my analyses kept revealing the contradictions within this system of thinking: the more the respondents sought union, the more their differences were revealed and congealed. Bringing into view the opposition of union and disunion and the limits of the aspiration to union, deconstructive analysis displaced this mindset. For me, however, the effect of this displacement was not to weaken the desire for women's union but rather to help me approach it with an awareness of its limitations.

As was stated at the outset of this chapter, the intent of creative analyses is to invent alternatives both to dominant assumptions and to the researcher's own interpretations. The notion of 'invention' brings into question the validity of creative analyses. The four analytical methods that I employed in this study were all concerned with questions of meanings: mapping them, grounding them, localizing them, or displacing them. Meaning is something that is repeatedly invented and reinvented. In carrying out each of the four methods, I sought to conform to our view of validity as integrity (see Chapter 4), in part by applying a standard appropriate to the method, whether coherence, empirical fit, contextualization, or exhaustion of the underlying assumption. The result, I would assert, is the emergence of valid contradictions within the analysis.

By building a self-contradictory process into the analytical approach, a researcher can promote critical analysis and responsible use of power at the stage when the research is most likely to become cut off from 'inclusive communities'. Each of the four methods of analysis adhered to one of our principles for ensuring that creative analyses promote empowerment. Creative analyses foster 'inclusive communities' by distinguishing rather than subsuming people's positions, by remaining accountable to rather than detached from those whose positions are being interpreted, by understanding rather than rejecting positions, and by inviting reflection rather than arriving at any one final position.

Most important, though, creative analyses are social action: they are not simply a way of analyzing the world, but a way of changing it. Whether or not researchers make room for them in their work, contradictions cannot be escaped; the discursive worlds we inhabit are shot through with contradictions that affect the terms on which we live our lives, how we perceive ourselves and our worlds. Nevertheless, people can effect change by speaking with each other about their experiences, gaining a wider perspective, uncovering their assumptions, and opening the way for alternative ways of life. Even though, far from proving the superiority of one position, the creative analyses involved in research as empowerment open up multiple understandings, they can still lead to social action. In this case, I was able to offer recommendations for shelters that were interested in unionizing. I was also able to contextualize the process of unionization within a larger political analysis of power. The participants in this study demonstrated commitment and creativity in their efforts to advance the empowerment of women and children in a violent and misogynistic society. Listening to their voices, I was able to move beyond the dichotomy of women's union/disunion and to develop four positions, thus filling in each corner of the square. My hope, though, is that shelter participants and others dedicated to empowerment can move beyond the confines of this square and invent a far fuller range of alternatives, encompassing and surpassing the elusive dream of women's union. In the words of Michelle Fine (1992: 23), 'acting in discourses' is a way to 'reframe what is as it activates images of what could be'.

Note

[1] Earlier versions of this chapter were presented at the May 1992 Annual Conference of the Canadian Women's Studies Association, Charlottetown, PEI; and at the June 1992 Annual Conference of the National Women's Studies Association, Austin, Texas.

7

Unity, Disruption, Transformation

We began this volume by asking how empowerment can serve as a framework for social research when it is not something that we can do 'for' or 'to' others. From the outset we indicated that research takes place in the context of the power exerted as both material and discursive forces within, between, and around the researchers and the researched. At the same time, we stressed that research as empowerment makes space for people's subjectivities (what they want 'for' themselves) and social change (what is to be done 'to' the world) by treating power as both its subject of analysis and its vehicle for change.

Throughout this volume we have presented examples of research done with various communities and emphasized that a strategy of 'links and interruptions' can help to counter the pressures that work to compress women into a conglomerate irrespective of their multiple identities. In particular, our illustrations have pointed to the relevance of research as empowerment for studying violence against women and children and for building democratic relations. In both cases, the use and misuse of power must be analyzed in ways that take into account both the material and the discursive forces at work. To work against violence or for democracy requires that social activists be united in their efforts to disrupt hegemonic material and discursive formations, and simultaneously develop both the social relations and the language necessary for social transformation.

The theoretical framework proposed in this book, combining feminism with postmodernism, focuses attention on both the material and the discursive dimensions of power. We understand the wariness of some feminists with respect to postmodernism, an area that in its focus on discourse can seem detached from political action and counter-productive to efforts to advance the interests of women as subjects. Yet as feminists we have found that incorporating postmodern insights into our political stance has allowed us to move our conceptualization of empowerment beyond an individualistic or humanistic notion of empowering others—of doing 'to' or 'for' them. It has made it possible for us to acknowledge complexity, diversity, and incompatibility without losing sight of the feminist objective of advancing women as a group. In providing detailed discussions of our own research projects, we have opened up our work for scrutiny and revealed the challenges and strengths of this approach to social inquiry, which includes building unity ('inclusive communities') while disrupting fixed ideas and normative categories; making links with communities ('validity' and 'reflexivity'); analyzing the power relations ('power plays') that weave through our work for social action; and interrupting hegemonic thinking to create 'alternative truths' ('creative analyses').

We work from a feminist perspective that includes a willingness to interrogate the foundations and boundaries of various feminisms, as well as our disciplinary foundations of social work and community psychology. Thus we agree with Angela McRobbie's (1993) blending of feminism and postmodernism, which offers many possibilities for praxis:

> Postmodernism does not mean that we have to do away with the subject but rather that we ask after the process of its construction. The value of postmodernism therefore is that, like deconstruction, it shows clearly how arguments bury opposition, its disorderly force is rude and impertinent in that it shows where power resides, hidden and quiet and displeased at being exposed. *Demonstrating these ruses does not mean descending into unruly chaos.* Rather it allows for open debate and dispute about boundaries and disciplines and what constitutes a study, what is knowledge. . . . Within feminism there is a need to speak as and for women but no sooner is this done than it is objected to. *This is the point at which things move* (p. 137; italics added) .

In this final chapter, we will discuss the implications of research as empowerment for working in a social and political context characterized by discursive conditions that operate against it. In particular, we will look at the backlash discourse that has been mobilized against feminist research on violence (a discourse to which research as empowerment is in part a response); the impact of discursive conditions on access to services; and, finally, how an empowerment approach can improve researchers' relations with funders by reshaping the discourses through which they communicate.

ADDRESSING CURRENT CONDITIONS

Backlash Discourse on Violence

Although the literature on violence against women and children has expanded greatly over the last twenty years, many feminists active in the field acknowledge several limitations in much of this literature. In many cases, for instance, research has focused on the experiences of white women and children, heterosexuals, and able-bodied people; has failed to explore the ways in which the larger social context affects the impact of violence on an individual; has not examined the effects of experiencing multiple forms of violence over a lifetime; and has not recognized the links between the many forms of violence (i.e., Canadian Panel on Violence Against Women, 1993; Goodman, Koss, Fitzgerald, Felipe-Russo, and Keita, 1993; Herman, 1992; Koss, 1990). Although our own disciplines of social work and psychology are heavily implicated in generating an ethnocentric and fragmented perspective on violence, they also show some promising trends towards more critical analyses that identify the material and discursive forces at work.

For example, some social-work researchers (Callahan, 1993; Swift, 1991) have shown how the legal, administrative, and practical contexts of child welfare disempower workers and clients alike by holding individual women accountable for the care of children while obscuring the impact of the social conditions that set children and their caregivers at risk of isolation and abuse. Increasingly, social workers are turning to feminist, First Nations, and community-based discourses for rethinking child welfare (e.g., Kérisit and St-Amand, 1995; Pennell and Burford, 1994) that foster the well-being of all children and their families, instead of protecting a minority of children from their parents (Wharf, 1993). Within psychology, the American Psychological Association Task Force on male violence against women has made several recommendations that support collaborative feminist approaches to research and are consistent with our empowerment framework as a way of addressing the limitations of mainstream research on violence. In their chapter 'Call For Action', Koss, Goodman, Browne, Fitzgerald, Keita, and Felipe Russo (1994: 239) make recommendations for the 'development of new research partnerships among psychological researchers, activists and victims before research is undertaken so that research questions and hypotheses will reflect the priorities and issues of concern to the victim as well as to psychologists' and for 'funding mechanisms that encourage collaboration'. In fact, Canada has recently funded five Family Violence Research Centres with specific mandates to engage in collaborative research programs. These are to be partnerships between communities and academics to ensure that research is designed to serve the needs of communities. Such encouraging trends have the potential to support the approaches to research outlined in this book.

At the same time, research on violence has been attacked by many conservative writers who dispute the statistical claims of feminist researchers. John Fekete, in his book *Moral panic: Biopolitics rising*, suggests that feminists are creating a 'moral panic' by generating implausible statistics that serve their own agenda. He questions the validity of qualitative interviews: 'StatsCan interviewers ask a leading question, bonding with the interviewee, women to woman, and signaling what is the rational position that they—and "us"—can share' (1994: 63). And he argues that feminist discourse cannot account for instances where women are violent towards men: 'women are victims of the system, and accountable for nothing. Anything they may do in response is either a manifestation of their vulnerability or an example of fighting back' (1994: 96). Similarly, Katie Roiphe (1993), a self-defined feminist, disputes the claims of research on date rape. Accusing feminists of creating 'date rape hype' that reinforces the status of women as victims and emphasizes women's fragility, she sees a cult of victimhood: 'there is power to be drawn from declaring one's victimhood and oppression' (Roiphe quoted in Faludi, 1995: 37). Authors like Camille Paglia (1994), Christina Hoff Sommers (1995), and most recently Donna Laframboise (1996) make similar claims about feminist research and discourse on violence against women, suggesting that women are presented only as victims when they too can be perpetrators of violence; and they critique slogans such as 'no means no' for ignoring grey areas in dating situations. According to Roiphe, 'There is a gray area in which someone's rape may be another person's bad night' (quoted in Faludi, 1995: 37). While we do not support the political perspective of these backlash writers whose intent is not to eradicate violence but to debunk feminism, their remarks do in some ways point to the cracks in the 'grand narrative' that has been created to explain violence against women.

We see our approach to research as a way of resisting these critiques and yet addressing some of the underlying questions that they can raise for feminists. In particular, these writers have pointed to feminists' reluctance to examine women as perpetrators and men as victims of violence. They do so within a heterosexist context and with a political intent that is hostile to feminism. Yet, however offensive they are, these writings raise some probing questions: How can we theorize and understand examples of violence where women are the perpetrators? Does our current discourse let us speak about women who abuse their children or their elderly relatives? Or lesbians who experience abuse within their relationships? Or, for that matter, gay men who are sexually assaulted by straight men? We want to ensure that our research methodology questions the gaps in and assumptions behind current knowledge. We are reminded of some of the questions we brought forward in Chapter 1, where we asked what assumptions about the causes and effects of violence, the perpetrators and victims of it, can be seen in the way we talk about and research violence, and what patterns of language serve to perpetuate oppressive power relations. The following example from Janice's work on the CLOSE project (Chapter 4) shows the need for an empowerment approach to research that considers the impacts of discourse.

THE CLOSE PROJECT: THE IMPACT OF DISCURSIVE CONDITIONS

In our work with shelters we realized that we needed to pay attention to discursive as well as material conditions if our training program on lesbian abuse was to make a significant change in service delivery. Most respondents to our needs assessment suggested that lesbians were welcome to use the services of shelters and residential second-stage housing programs, since their mandate is to provide services to all abused women. None of the services, however, specifically noted in their brochures that lesbians were welcome, nor did they include lesbians as part of their public education or outreach work. The following comments from the needs assessment, taken from our final report (Balan, Chorney, and Ristock, 1995), reflect the tendency of many shelters to see their use of language as adequate and inclusive, and hence to believe that their approach to addressing violence is not heterosexist or racist:

> We don't have a flashing neon sign you know. In our public education we say all women are welcome—that would include lesbians. We would rarely turn anyone away.

> We don't put brochures out that are specifically geared to women in lesbian battering relationships. There isn't anything either that would give the message 'don't call us'. We just refer to women in general.

> The issue would be that there's violence and safety, it wouldn't matter whether she was lesbian or native . . . so it really hasn't been an issue here. If a woman came to us and was lesbian, we would deal with her the same as we would deal with any other female.

These comments reflect the way the hegemonic discourse about violence against women—that it is committed by men—manages to subsume subjectivities that might transgress or interrupt its domain without actually repressing or forbidding those subjectivities (Alcoff and Gray, 1993). Therefore it was important in our training work with these shelters to include the views of lesbians who experienced their assumptions as barriers to receiving services. Many lesbians spoke specifically about the discourse concerning violence that assumes heterosexuality and gave examples of how the language used on intake forms in social services perpetuates this assumption:

> The forms deny my partner as being family, her role seems to always be 'OTHER'.

> Forms lack a place for sexual orientation . . . have to fit under marital status.

> My partner is not considered as family, not acknowledged 'cause forms aren't inclusive.

Like Patti Lather (1986), we see research as empowerment as both encouraging reflection and understanding among participants and contributing to theoretical knowledge. Based on some of the comments from the evaluation of the training, we feel that our approach was transformational in bringing forward voices that are normally subsumed and in the process enabling participants to become more aware of the complex material and discursive conditions of their work.

> While of course this issue is prevalent in all relationships, perhaps I believed the myth that women are gentler (in control) by nature. How sad to realize we are not.

> While I feel I have a fairly good understanding of [lesbian abuse and homophobia], I believe that this will be an ongoing learning process which will help me in the work I do, but also ensure that I and my staff receive ongoing training in abuse in lesbian relationships and how our services can be made accessible.

FUNDING STRATEGIES

Discursive conditions affected the CLOSE project in another way as well. We received government funding for our project from the federal Family Violence Initiative, but the funders revealed that this was one of the riskiest projects receiving their support. Fortunately, their definition of violence was broad enough to include same-sex domestic violence, but that breadth was permitted with much trepidation in the context of virulently anti-lesbian and anti-gay rhetoric from various religious leaders and politicians. This case shows the effect of discursive forces on material conditions. Research as empowerment is concerned with showing how violence, social issues, and research practices are discursively as well as materially constructed. We see this methodology as having the potential to offer the richest understanding of issues and hence the most solid base for taking appropriate action.

To carry out any study, funding is usually required. Applying for and receiving funds can at times compromise or threaten the directions of a research project. If the funders for the CLOSE Project had been unwilling to take the risk of funding research on lesbian abuse, the project might not have been undertaken at all, or only in a far less thorough fashion. In an earlier chapter, Janice noted that funders can restrict research by narrowing the areas for investigation or imposing deadlines for submission of reports. Joan has experienced similar problems with funders. Our focus here, though, is on using research as empowerment to reconstruct relationships with funders. We present two examples from Joan's research. The first, from a collaborative research project on single mothers pursuing post-secondary education, called Hoops and Hurdles, shows how participants were able to work within an empowerment framework despite the demands and discourses of funders that both resisted and supported collaborative approaches; it also shows how a community-building approach can bring together participants' aspirations and funders' expectations and keep the research 'grounded' in the participants' realities. The second example concerns a project to evaluate a young people's program where government funders *supported* an empowerment approach. It shows how the team used democratic decision-making to exert the organization's control over a study with the potential to undermine its funding. We refer to this strategy *vis-à-vis* the public funder as 'owning the study'. Both examples reveal the difficulties that have to be negotiated when working in an empowerment context and receiving external funding.

1. Grounding the Research: The Hoops and Hurdles Project

> Projects were evaluated in light of their capacity 1) to demonstrate . . . principles of social participation and social investment and 2) to contribute to a cumulative knowledge base which could be applied in policy and program development. . . . 'Hoops and Hurdles' represents the most integrated collaboration of all the projects (Pearson, 1994: 4).

Grounding the research: ensuring that the study remains based in the research participants' realities. At the same time, researchers need to demonstrate the authenticity and relevance of the project in terms comprehensible to its funders.

Carried out in Newfoundland, the Canadian province with the lowest literacy rate, the Hoop and Hurdles Project focused on the importance of education for advancing sole-support mothers' economic position. In developing a lobbying strategy on this issue, an organization called Single Moms Against Poverty recognized that its efforts could be reinforced by documenting the situation of students who were single mothers. As Cathy, the organization's president, explained, such research would provide the legitimacy required for policy-makers to act. Thus, when approached by several members of social-work faculty at Memorial University to take part in the Hoops and Hurdles Project, Single Moms Against Poverty agreed. One of the faculty members, Sharon, had been a founding member of Single Moms Against Poverty, and because of her involvement the organization was confident that the research would be attuned to its philosophy and agenda for change. Together, the academics and Single Moms Against Poverty put forward a successful proposal to a funding competition held by the federal National Welfare Grants program. The objectives of the project fitted well with NWG's priority on developing strategies for overcoming child and family poverty.

The study employed a community-building model developed by Sharon (Taylor, 1994). The aim of this model is to reorganize society so that resources can be equitably distributed and communities become safe, democratic, and self-sustaining; its method is to mobilize various sectors of society to participate in this reconstructive process. Adoption of the community-building model meant that the Hoops and Hurdles Project was designed in a sequential and collaborative manner. Each stage of the research built on the study's prior findings. This was achieved by mobilizing the participation of diverse groups through three structures: a community-building team, a research team, and a steering committee. The community-building team, consisting of students and single mothers, along with Sharon, set the vision for the research; collected the data through interviews and focus groups; and analyzed the findings and disseminated them through media such as workshops, a video, and a manual. The second group, the research team, included the academics and representatives from Single Moms Against Poverty and was the entity through which the money from the funding body was channelled. The research team, responsible for ensuring that the study met the terms set out in the agreement with the funders, served largely as consultants on research methodology, although they also took part in preparing academic-style reports. The third body, the steering committee, brought together the community-building and research teams with a wider group of community representatives from single-mothers' organizations on and off campus and from academic and government departments. Although this collaborative structure was encouraged by the funders, it also gave rise to some uncertainties.

The community-building approach meant that participants were both numerous and widely dispersed, and made for a rapidly accelerating momentum. From the funders' perspective, this process ensured that the project had the 'social participation and social investment' necessary for strong provincial and community support. In fact, National Welfare Grants had encouraged collaborative proposals precisely because these were seen as actively involving Canadians in identifying their social needs and determining solutions to them. However, the community-building approach also had a 'down side', according to Fran, an NWG representative. As she explained, 'it was difficult to see clearly the structure and the logical progression of the project because it seemed to evolve and grow in new and different directions.' At the same time, she recognized that the funders could remain connected with the Hoops and Hurdles Project because of its community-building strategy. Referring to a meeting between the funders and project participants, she observed: 'The participation of the mothers was a plus. Hearing their stories again grounded the research from my point of view.' This meeting served not only to ground the research for the funding body but to make the latter's mandate and requirements clear to the participants.

Connecting with life experiences of single mothers

At this meeting, the three representatives from Single Moms Against Poverty—Cathy, Pat, and Trudy—relayed once again their life stories. They were applying to the funders the same principles of community-building that they used with single mothers to break their isolation. Looking back on the meeting, research team and steering committee members agreed that the three women had told their stories in a sincere, controlled, and intense manner, speaking not for effect but out of their own real experience, with the result that listeners were moved to connect at a personal level with the mission of the study. The direct involvement of community groups, NWG recognized, ensured an 'integrated response' in which service deliverers and service recipients exchanged ideas and jointly developed programming (Pearson, 1994: 7). The Hoops and Hurdles Project's 'participatory action research approach', Fran noted, 'ensured authenticity and relevance in terms of the subjects' concerns and issues.'

Translating life experiences into funders' language

At this same meeting, the funding representatives asked some very direct questions about the study's methodology and, in particular, the objectivity of advocacy research. They wanted a clear explanation of how the research would produce findings with the validity necessary to influence policy and program development. A long-time representative of National Welfare Grants, named Evariste, who had not been present at the meeting but was informed about the project, later reviewed NWG's position. He stressed that NWG had had a long-term commitment to supporting the development of research infrastructures promoting citizens' involvement, and viewed participatory action research as a viable route to this end. However, NWG also had had to address the issue of the 'public perception' of such research: any loss of its credibility would weaken its capacity to influence policy-makers. What became evident was that funders were constructing 'collaboration' in a way that could be at odds with an empowerment framework. In other words, the funders wanted participation, but were reluctant to bring 'marginal' voices into the research process.

In response to the question of validity, initially some team members asserted that the intent of the research was not to be 'objective': rather, its validity depended on its adopting the specific standpoint of the women concerned. Recognizing that the group was reaching an impasse in language,

Joan categorized the methodology as 'objective' and went on to define the meaning of this term in the context of action research. She explained that the research had an overt mission—the empowerment of single-mother students—but that adherence to this mission did not mean that the researchers would obscure or mask inconvenient findings. Instead, they would consider all the data and interpret them in a manner that promoted a responsible strategy for advancing the interests of single-mother students. The community-building approach of the study ensured that these decisions would not be made in isolation; instead, the perspectives of a wide range of participants would be incorporated in an 'objective' assessment of the data. In later feedback, other participants told Joan that she had translated the group's statements in a manner that made sense to the funding body, without contravening the principles behind the project.

Grounding the research for all project participants

Both the public funder and the project members had to alter their discourse according to the expectations placed upon them. The question posed by such alterations is how much of the original meaning is translated into the new language and how much is lost in the process of translation. National Welfare Grants, through its 'integrated response', and the Hoops and Hurdles Project, through its community-building approach, both sought to promote inclusive dialogue and co-operative planning. In so doing, they moved grass-roots organizations out of isolation, or what Linda Briskin (1991) refers to as a posture of 'disengagement', and into the mainstream. In the Hoops and Hurdles Project, this meant explaining both single mothers' perspectives and the collaborative research methodology in a language comprehensible to the government funder.

This translation gained continued financial support for the Hoops and Hurdles Project. Similar strategies have been employed by many feminist groups across Canada. As Jill Vickers (1991) points out, Canadian feminists are more likely than their counterparts in the United States to accept (or obtain) state support, particularly in the area of social welfare. At the same time, Canadian feminists have recognized the dangers of depending on government funding and have sought to minimize its effects on their priorities. To prevent groups from competing for government support, a particularly effective strategy has been to form coalitions to collectively request and deliver funds according to members' needs (see Hoehne, 1988). An integrated response and a community-building strategy are both ways of building coalitions that help to keep advocacy groups from being deflected away from their aims and into battles among themselves. The Hoops and Hurdles researchers attended to the voices on the margin while making these voices understandable to others.

> **Owning the study:** occurs when all participants share their knowledge and reach key decision through consensus. With this sense of ownership, the research group can together decide how the research is to be carried out and how its findings are to be interpreted, released, and used.

2. Owning the Externally Funded Study: The 'Choices for Youth' Evaluation

This evaluation occurred during a period of cost-cutting by the government of Newfoundland, whose already small tax base was facing further erosion as a result of the depletion of Atlantic cod stocks. The necessity of programming for young people gained prominence through the widely publicized hearings (Hughes, 1991) into cover-ups of widespread physical and sexual child abuse committed by Christian Brothers at Mount Cashel Orphanage in the 1970s. Even though the charges did not involve anyone currently working at the facility, the Brothers decided to shut it down. This imminent closure led the Department of Social Services and specifically its Division of Child Welfare, the provincial authority responsible for the welfare of the young people affected, to form a committee to plan the phase-out (Lynch et al., 1991; Sullivan, Fildes, and Turner, 1993). Riding the wave of public concern, the Division of Child Welfare took a bold new direction in the way it organized and constituted the planning committee and its working group. They hired as consultants and appointed as committee members people who were strongly committed to developing collective organizations and incorporating feminist perspectives into child welfare. They also organized a larger planning committee that included residents of the orphanage to form a new non-profit community-living program called 'Choices for Youth'. Its philosophy of empowerment emphasized the importance of ensuring that young people had a say in the program and some control over their lives.

From the outset, the plan was to conduct an evaluation of the program within two years of its initiation. An open and thorough evaluation was seen as a way of forestalling the secrecy that had concealed the abuse at Mount Cashel and of helping the program to keep on track with its original objectives. It was also recognized that a positive evaluation would help to legitimize the program and bolster its image with its government funder. As a publicly funded agency just establishing itself in a time of government retrenchment, Choices had good reason to fear the consequences of an evaluation, especially since by now public attention to Mount Cashel was dwindling. Moreover, having accepted money from the Department of Social Services to carry out the evaluation, Choices knew that the Treasury Board would very likely act on its findings. Given its dependence on state support,

Choices realized that government was the ultimate owner not only of the evaluation but of the organization itself, no matter how empowering and collaborative it meant to be. Nevertheless, Choices developed a strategy that served to offset the government's ownership to some extent.

In part, this was feasible precisely because the project committee originally established by the Division of Child Welfare had encouraged such a strategy in the formulation of the organization's philosophy and structure. Then, in keeping with the project's philosophy, the Division of Child Welfare departed from normal practices to route the funds for the evaluation directly through the program to be evaluated. More often, empowerment projects are subject to external evaluation, with the result that, despite a language of empowerment, it suddenly becomes all too clear that the funders, and not the project participants, own the project and the future of empowerment efforts is out of the hands of the people directly concerned. Being 'allowed' to run its own evaluation made it possible for Choices to work with evaluators of its choosing. Accordingly, an evaluation team was formed consisting of three evaluators and six representatives of Choices for Youth (one young person, four staff, and one board member). Their ability to take charge of the evaluation was strengthened by their combining representative and consensual decision-making.

The evaluators conducted individual and/or group interviews with residents, staff, parents, and community representatives, and analyzed the young people's files and other agency documents. Throughout the interviews with the evaluation team, the theme of 'owning the evaluation' recurred as members talked about the necessity of adhering to collective decision-making. This joint decision-making was seen as crucial in order to respect the privacy, dignity, and self-determination of the young people while at the same time ensuring that the evaluation was thorough and offered a basis from which to improve the program. (As the evaluation team recognized, to obtain informed and voluntary consent from the young people required more than simply presenting them with a consent form outlining the terms for their being interviewed or having their personal files read by the evaluators; see Appendix IV. It also meant that the three evaluators met with the young people before the evaluation began to outline its purpose and process and to listen to their concerns and suggestions.)

The Choices team members wanted an honest appraisal, but they also wanted one that would portray the current strengths and future potential of this fledgling program rather than undermine its credibility with its funding body, the Department of Social Services. In the language of the program-evaluation literature (Herman, Morris, and Fitz-Gibbon, 1987), they were asking for a 'formative evaluation', aimed at assessing how a program is operating in order to revamp it as needed, rather than a 'summative evaluation', aimed at judging whether a program warrants continued support. In agreement with the Choices' representatives, the evaluators stressed that the study should focus on the fact that the program was not only relatively new but pioneering an innovative approach and structure within the social-welfare system.

More than a year after the study was completed, Joan interviewed members of the evaluation team about their experiences. The accounts that follow, provided by representatives of all five groups involved, point to the empowering, progressive work that was possible even within the difficult context of producing a program evaluation for the funders in a time of cutbacks; they also illustrate the depth and comprehensiveness that comes from including diverse perspectives on an evaluation team.

Owning the evaluation

Young person: Despite his concerns that the work would be too complicated and the language over his head, Greg accepted a staff member's invitation to join the evaluation committee because of his strong commitment to the young people at Choices. Seeing himself above all as 'watch-dog', he wanted to make sure the evaluation did not 'fool it up [cause problems] for others' in the program. Although he would soon be turning 21 and graduating from the care of the child-welfare system, he knew that Choices was a good program and wanted the evaluation 'to come out the right way' so that it could continue. He wanted to help the other residents, even if he had to 'push [himself] to talk with people in positions of authority'.

Looking back on his work with the evaluation team, Greg noted with some surprise, 'I enjoyed it'. He saw the evaluation team as addressing 'pretty in-depth stuff' that was 'important' for Choices. He liked the fact that the issues were not 'pre-decided', and that decisions were worked out by the team and put into effect in a relatively short period of time.

Board member: Michelle, a counsellor in a program for children, young people, and their families, served as the co-chair of Choices' board of directors. Unlike Greg, she was quite familiar with program-evaluation methodology. She also recognized that a solid and creditable evaluation could help Choices to improve its services and to establish its trustworthiness in using public money.

Michelle saw the program as relatively unprepared for undergoing an evaluation, and thought that, as a consequence, the evaluators were forced to give the team a 'crash course' on the subject. Since the organization itself did not have 'fully articulated' indicators of empowerment, she appreciated the fact that the evaluators took the time to 'fish around' for and 'construct' statements of goals and tasks congruent with the organization's philosophy. Although negotiating the evaluation measures was time-consuming, she

believed that 'the substantial investment at the front end helped with ownership of the data at the end'.

Michelle stressed that the evaluation did not end when the evaluators
submitted their final report. The Choices team refused to release the report
for almost a year, until they had closely reviewed the findings and abstracted
areas for action. She estimated that the organization put in easily twice as
much time on analyzing the report after the evaluators had left as they had
on the actual planning of the evaluation. The team took the time to map out
its blueprint for change even though the delay in releasing the report created some tension with their government funders. The funders then had to be
convinced that this evaluation should be treated as a formative exercise that
presumed program continuance rather than a summative study that could
threaten the autonomy of the collaborative organization.

Live-in staff: A relief worker, Andy was a member of the staff who lived in the
apartments with the young people, and along with one full-time worker, he
represented the live-in staff on the evaluation team. Although he appreciated
the 'mutual learning' that took place, he was disappointed by the 'lack of
answers' in the evaluators' final report, which he saw as inadequate in its
identification of and attention to internal organizational problems. As he
bluntly stated, he had wanted the evaluation to hold 'empowered staff
accountable'. He was pleased, though, with the evaluation report as a 'tool for
communicating with the Department of Social Services'.

Office staff: The office staff were represented on the evaluation team by a co-
ordinator, Jackie, and a counsellor, Diane. Diane had not only worked at
Mount Cashel but been a part of the planning committee for Choices; in her
eyes, the evaluation was a way of 'following through' to see if everything they
had wanted to achieve had been accomplished. Like the other Choices participants, both Jackie and Diane stressed the way Choices took ownership of
the evaluation. Diane commented that the report 'felt like ours', and that the
organization developed a 'good process' for handling the report. Jackie con-
curred, and stressed the seriousness with which diverse Choices members
approached this task. As she explained, the program stakeholders (board,
staff, young people, and community representatives) read the report with a
'critical eye', discussed what was not accurate, and pulled out recommendations for improvement to be further addressed by program committees.
Their main disappointment was that the funding body did not appear to have
given the evaluation the same degree of thought they had.

Evaluators: Gale and Joan were the two university-based evaluators. Neither
felt that the involvement of Choices members with a stake in ensuring future
funding, or their desire to 'own' the evaluation, compromised the validity or
rigour of the evaluation process. As Gale pointed out, few programs, unless

supported by federal funding, ventured to take such a hard look at what they were doing. At the same time, he was aware that the Division of Child Welfare was proud of this new organization and its own role in establishing an innovative and positive response to the closure of Mount Cashel. Both of them saw the collaborative planning process, although time-consuming, as making for a far stronger evaluation design, and hence more valid and useful findings. Significantly, neither worried that the collaborative planning would prevent them from making an independent appraisal of the organization; instead, they saw it as helping them to carry out an evaluation within this specific organizational context.

While the team members saw themselves as responsible for representing particular constituencies or interests, they were also aware of contributing to a collectively owned decision process. With this sense of joint ownership, the desire expressed by Greg, 'not [to] let them fool it up for the others' did not turn into obstructive protectionism, but rather became a resolve shared by all evaluation team members to make sure that the evaluation was carried out the right way. The sense of joint ownership also meant that 'following through' went well beyond collecting and analyzing data, to determining how the findings were to be interpreted, used, and released. From this position of strength, Choices was able to advance action plans in partnership with a government division that had a significant commitment to making this program work. In the end, although Choices did not entirely own the evaluation, it had much more control over it than is usually the case in such situations. It could exert this control because its philosophy of empowerment applied not only to the young people but to the program as a whole.

Contradictions in Funding

The funding that makes much empowerment research feasible also brings its own set of contradictions. As the two examples above have revealed, research participants and funding agents alike recognized that the studies in question could be used to discredit the programs and reduce their capacity to support empowerment approaches. The Choices evaluation team worried that the funding department might use the findings to assert greater control over the organization and thus threaten its ability to carry out an empowerment program for young people. In the case of the Hoops and Hurdles Project, National Welfare Grants pointed out that the advocacy methodology of the study could diminish its credibility and erode NWG's own capacity to fund future participatory studies. In each instance both the funders and the recipients took risks, but not without strategies calculated to mediate them.

Rather than refuse the money for the evaluation, Choices used democratic decision-making to strengthen its control over the process. The diversity of perspectives and locations in the evaluation increased the accountability and validity of the empowerment aspect of the evaluation. The funding body played a contradictory role in supporting this process because of the attention it gave to the young people concerned while not necessarily giving the final report the weight the participants had hoped for. Instead of rejecting the Hoops and Hurdles program's application for funds, National Welfare Grants pushed the project participants to justify why it should continue to receive funding. In turn, the community-building process of the project strengthened the group while making it possible to reach out to the funding body. To make itself intelligible to the funders, the group had to adopt their language. At the same time, the commitment to inclusiveness led the group to attend to voices of marginalized groups.

The negotiations show that it is possible to gain funding for an empowerment approach. However, participants must be clear about the principles they want to maintain. Both examples show that, with negotiation, funders were able to support an empowerment research process. Their discourse of collaboration is not necessarily shared by those working in an empowerment framework; yet precisely because of the funders' emphasis on collaboration, research participants were able not only to get the funds, but also, perhaps, to disrupt fixed notions of what constitutes good research and programming. These examples again show the transformative possibilities of working from an empowerment approach that acknowledges both discursive and material contexts.

CONCLUSIONS

At the time of writing, the highly publicized O.J. Simpson trial has just ended in acquittal. In this trial we have seen instances of violence against women represented through 911 tapes of Nicole Simpson pleading for help; of research findings mediated through the experts who presented various tangible samples of 'evidence' for the courts; of feminism in the startling prospect of Lenore Walker, feminist psychologist and battered-women's advocate, using the authority of her research to testify for the defence (though in the event she did not appear); of racism in the *Time* magazine cover of an altered (darkened) photograph of O.J. Simpson. We read the results of many opinion polls before the verdict that showed people divided along racial lines on the question of guilt or innocence. As we conclude our work, we wonder how we can understand this. What new questions in our processes of social inquiry do we need to ask? How can we best do research so that it is committed to emancipatory agendas: advocacy-based, yet building theory? The Simpson case exemplifies many issues that we struggle with in research: the constructedness of 'truth'; the difference that social difference makes to 'truth'; the breakdown of traditional, objective means of deducing 'truth'. Against the social backdrop of this case, we are reminded of why we have insisted on 'links and interruptions' as the sustaining culture for research as empowerment.

We have argued that a more collaborative, consultative approach to critical research is needed. We place research participants at the centre of this process as a way of building knowledge and engaging in social action. We see transformative possibilities as arising both within the consciousness of individuals and within communities. We are committed to furthering this work, to taking our research into many different and contradictory directions, to revealing the ins and outs of research practices. We resist establishing any new research orthodoxies while hoping that we can contribute to more interesting and useful ways of knowing (Lather, 1986). We do this because we are committed to a view of empowerment that stems from agency, not the agency of an essential inner self waiting to be empowered, but of a self working with others to negotiate the terms of its own emergence. As Audre Lorde (1984) writes: 'Our acts against oppression become integral with self, motivated and empowered from within.' We hope our readers too will engage in research as an empowering act, as a way of uniting people working for social change, disrupting restrictive ways of thinking, and transforming the social world.

Glossary

This glossary indicates the general manner in which we are using terms in this volume. It is undertaken with the recognition that definitions are always elusive; as contexts vary, so do meanings.

'Alternative truths' — other knowledges constructed through research as empowerment.

Binarism — a system of thought in which one concept is defined by contrasting it with its opposite (e.g., male/female) and their differences are used to elevate one over the other.

Collective — a non-hierarchical, usually small organization in which the workers exercise control and make decisions by consensus.

Construction — a term used to counter the notion that objects in the social world have an intrinsic meaning, and to convey the view that social categories are created and given meaning through social forces that construct an idea.

Creative analyses — thinking outside the confines of dominant assumptions and the researcher's own interpretations, to invent alternative truths.

Deconstruction — analysis that takes apart socially constructed categories as a way of seeing how a particular world is constructed.

Discourse — a set of assumptions, socially shared and often unconscious, reflected in language, that positions people who speak within them and frames knowledge.

Discourse analysis — analysis that examines language and ideologies as a way of understanding how meanings are produced.

Discursive conditions — non-material conditions relating to language and ideologies.

Disruption — resistance against hegemonic control that interrupts pre-set ways of thinking and offers new routes of possible action.

Empowerment — the process and product of bringing people together in such a way that they can critically analyze and responsibly use power within particular contexts.

Epistemology — the study of what knowledge is and how it is created.

Essentialism — the belief that a category (such as woman abuse) is real and always encompasses certain essential or necessary properties.

Feminisms — a term used to convey the diversity within feminist theoretical and political views on understanding the oppression of women.

Feminist empiricism — an epistemology in the positivist tradition which claims that feminist research is more objective than its traditional counterpart because it is not skewed by androcentric bias.

Feminist postmodernism — a variant of postmodern epistemology which claims that feminist research exposes male/female binarism and advances more open and responsive discourses.

Feminist standpoint theory — an epistemology in the Hegelian/Marxist traditions, which claims that feminist research yields a more moral and comprehensive understanding than its traditional counterpart by achieving a feminist standpoint based on women's struggles against oppression.

Foundationalism — a modern epistemology that posits the autonomous and rational individual as the foundation for discerning universal truths. It encompasses both of the dominant streams of research: quantitative (positivistic) and qualitative (interpretive).

Hegemony — the construction and imposition of unified thinking that serves the interests of dominant groups, homogenizes difference, and disadvantages non-dominant groups.

Identity — the social self that is named and experienced. Identity is socially constructed and includes social positions such as gender, race, and sexuality. Compare *Subjectivity*.

'Inclusive communities' — created by bringing together people from diverse backgrounds and social positions and constructing a firm identity as participants in a process based on respecting separate identities.

Location — the position of researchers, identified in terms not only of who they are, but of why they are doing the research, and what their subjectivities bring to the work.

Material conditions — conditions that are tangible and concrete (e.g., economic, structural)

Ontology — the study of the nature of existence and reality.

Participatory action — a research methodology that seeks to create usable knowledge by involving the people researched as researchers in social analysis and action.

Performance a postmodern term used to reflect the notion that categories such as race, gender, and sexuality (whether seen as constructed or essential) are unstable and ultimately unknowable. Therefore acts engaged in to disclose identity are seen as performances that also maintain and create identity categories. To acknowledge the performance is a way of beginning to dismantle the category.

Phenomenology — a philosophy which rejects the view that the world is naturally ordered and seeks to determine the universal structures (essences) of human consciousness and how people in relationship with phenomena intentionally give meaning to the world.

Positivism — an Enlightenment epistemology in which logical calculation and empirical observation, rather than tradition, are seen as the sources of valid and useful knowledge.

Postmodernisms — epistemologies which deny that human reason is impartial and transcendental and, in so doing, resist the tendency to create all-encompassing descriptions and explanations of social life.

Power — a relational force, not a fixed entity, that operates in all interactions. While it can be oppressive, power can also be enabling.

'Power plays' — the subjectivities, external demands, and social relations that must be negotiated throughout the process of research.

Praxis — the joining of theory and action so that each is informed by and changes through its relation with the other.

Reflexivity — awareness of how we as researchers observe and affect actions and discourse; how we attribute meaning and intentions; what understandings we are creating; and how we are creating them. Reflexivity also means being prepared to adjust our research methods to reflect what we learn both from the community and from our own reflections.

Responsibility — holding oneself morally accountable for one's actions.

Research — the search for answers to questions in a way that is made open to the appraisal of others.

Research as empowerment — an approach to research that seeks to effect empowerment at all stages of the research process through critical analysis and responsible use of power.

Subjectivity — the contingent and variable sense of self, conscious and unconscious, both as actor and as 'acted upon'.

Transparency — making the researcher visible in the research process.

Triangulation — using multiple methods to gain different perspectives on a subject.

Validity — the integrity, accountability, and value of a research project, achieved through accountability both to the participants and to those who will be affected by the outcome.

Appendix I

TRIANGULATION I:
DIFFERENT QUESTIONS, DIFFERENT METHODS

QUESTIONNAIRE ON FEMINIST COLLECTIVES

Please answer the following questions. Feel free to write any additional comments or explanations on the backs of these pages. Once again, I thank you for your participation in this study.

General information

1. Name of organization: _____

2. Briefly describe the mandate of your organization:

   _____

3. How many years has your organization operated as a feminist collective?
   _____ years/months

4. How many salaried collective members are presently employed?
   full-time: _____   part-time: _____   other: _____

   (Please explain) _____

5. Please state who is filling out this questionnaire: (e.g., full-time collective member; entire collective, etc.): _____

6. Briefly describe your organization's definition of a feminist collective:

   _____

7. Briefly describe how this feminist collective was formed:

   _____

8. What qualifications or qualities do you look for when hiring collective members?

   _____

Organizational structure

9. Does your organization have an executive director?

    Yes _____   No _____

    Comments: _____

10. Does your organization have a board of directors?

    Yes _____   No _____

    Comments: _____

11. Does your organization use volunteers?

    Yes _____   No _____

    Comments: _____

12. Does your organization receive government funding?

    Yes _____   No _____

    Comments: _____

13. Does your organization receive funding from other sources?

    Yes _____   No _____

    Comments: _____

14. Does your organization have charitable status?

    Yes _____   No _____

    Comments: _____

15. Is your organization unionized?

    Yes _____   No _____

    Comments: _____

16. Is your organization a member of any coalition groups and/or affiliated with any community and/or political/issue-oriented groups?

    Yes _____   No _____

    Please specify: _____

17. Is the public aware that you operate as a feminist collective?

Yes _____   No _____

Comments: _____

18. These questions attempt to understand your organization's structure, please comment on any other dimensions that you feel have been left out: _____

Funding

19. Describe your present funding situation; is it secure?

_____

20. How has your funding situation impacted on your organization?

_____

Collective Process

21. Which of the following processes does your organization take part in / practice? Please indicate either yes or no for each item:

Participatory decision-making	Yes _____	No _____
Decisions reached by consensus	Yes _____	No _____
Decisions reached by voting	Yes _____	No _____
Equal salaries within collective	Yes _____	No _____
Job responsibilities are shared	Yes _____	No _____
Job responsibilities are divided	Yes _____	No _____
Job responsibilities are rotated	Yes _____	No _____
Hiring and firing is done by collective	Yes _____	No _____
Hiring and firing is done by director or board	Yes _____	No _____
Regular collective meetings are held	Yes _____	No _____

Regular collective evaluations are
conducted   Yes _____ No _____

Day-to-day information is passed on
through a shift change and/or
through a log or journal   Yes _____ No _____

Please comment on other collective processes that your organization uses:

---

22. Which of the following difficulties do you feel your organization has experienced and would identify as a problem due to the collective structure:

Poor communication   Yes _____ No _____

Slowness in decision-making   Yes _____ No _____

Collective members have unequal
influence in group process   Yes _____ No _____

Value of acceptance from community/
government/other agencies   Yes _____ No _____

Varying degrees of commitment
and accountability in members   Yes _____ No _____

Tension/conflict with board or
director   Yes _____ No _____

Splits/factions within the collective   Yes _____ No _____

Conflict within collective   Yes _____ No _____

Please state any other difficulties or expand on your responses:

---

23. Has your collective relied on any of the following to resolve collectivedifficulties:

Mediator for conflict resolution   Yes _____ No _____

Facilitator to address issues   Yes _____ No _____

Retreats or gatherings to renew
the collective   Yes _____ No _____

Educational/informational workshop
sessions or conferences   Yes _____ No _____

Reading materials discussed with
the collective   Yes _____ No _____

Please state other responses used to deal with collective difficulties:

_____

24. Has your collective practised any of the following pressure tactics:

Letter-writing campaigns	Yes _____	No _____
Lobbying	Yes _____	No _____
Petitions	Yes _____	No _____
Background research/testimony	Yes _____	No _____
Legal action	Yes _____	No _____
Demonstrations	Yes _____	No _____
Endorsements given to political groups or causes	Yes _____	No _____

Comments: _____

Feminist ideology

25. Describe your organization's involvement with the women's movement:

_____

26. Explain your organization's reason for working as a feminist collective:

_____

27. Has your organization's adherence to feminism affected your service in any of the following ways:

It works through our collective and service provisions	Yes _____	No _____
It sets our organizational goals	Yes _____	No _____
It involves us in social change/action work	Yes _____	No _____
It involves us in policy and/or legal reform work	Yes _____	No _____
It provides us with an analysis and approach for working with our service recipients	Yes _____	No _____

Comments: _____

28. Please indicate whether the following statements reflect your organization's involvement with social change:

We act as role models for the women
we work with   Yes _____   No _____

We provide feminist analysis
that has an impact on women's lives   Yes _____   No _____

We see ourselves as a feminist
movement organization   Yes _____   No _____

We provide an alternative service   Yes _____   No _____

We are empowered by the work that
we do   Yes _____   No _____

We are involved in additional
political work   Yes _____   No _____

We will change the position of
women in our society through the
type of work that we are doing   Yes _____   No _____

Comments: _____

29. Does providing a social service while adhering to feminism pose any contradictions for you or your organization? Please comment on the contradictions:

_____

30. Please offer any other comments or suggestions that you think will aid me in my understanding of feminist collectives in the social sevices:

_____

Thank you! Please send the completed questionnaire along with your informational documents in the enclosed envelope as soon as possible.

DOCUMENT ANALYSIS

Name of Organization:

Location:

Type of Document:

Presence of values: Quote sentence from document

A. *Stated goals*

Goal of empowerment   _____

Goal of equality   _____

Goal of social change   _____

Comments on context or other goals:

_____

B. *Processes stated*

Process of women helping women   _____

Process of choice _____

Process of sharing _____

Process of non-judgemental services   _____

Comment on context or other processes cited:

_____

C. *Definition of service*

Service is defined as a collective   _____

Service is defined as feminist   _____

Service addresses the issue of violence against women in their documents:

_____

Comments on context of the service:

_____

INTERVIEW FRAMEWORK

Questions for Collective Workers

1. How many years have you been a part of this collective? what has this experience been like? Has your collective undergone changes since it first began or since you began working there?

2. Is it important for you to work collectively? Why? What are your reasons for working collectively? Do you think this structure works for social-service agencies?

3. What are some of the problems or difficulties that you have experienced working collectively—problems with consensus decision-making, differences in power, feminist ideology etc.?

4. What about contradictions in your work? Do you experience any? For example, between immediate social-service work and long-term social-change goals?

5. What about working with/across differences? Does your collective discuss issues of class, race, and sexual orientation? How are differences in power and privilege addressed when working in a structure that sees everyone asequal participants? How does your collective respond to power differentials?

6. What is your vision for yourself and for your collective? Where do you see this work going? How do you see this structure evolving?

7. Is there anything else that you would like to add that can help me better understand the workings of collectives and your experiences?

Appendix II

TRIANGULATION II:
DIFFERENT QUESTION, DIFFERENT METHODS

LESBIAN NEEDS ASSESSMENT

Questions Asked in Community Focus Groups / Questionnaires / Telephone Interviews

About social services generally:

1. Can you think of any community social services in your area that advertise, or in some other way make you feel they welcome lesbians and bisexual women? What are those services and how do they let you know that they welcome lesbians and bisexual women?

2. What is it like as a lesbian or bisexual woman to use, or try to use, community social services: for example, health services, legal services, child care etc.?

3. Is there anything missing for you in these services? What might stop you or other lesbians/bisexual women from using these services?

4. Do you know of any social-service agencies that have lesbians or bisexual women on staff? Do you think that makes a difference in whether or not lesbians or bisexual women use those services and what kind of service they receive?

I'd like to ask some questions that deal more specifically, with services for lesbians and bisexual women in abusive relationships with women. I'd like to share a definition of abuse we're using at CLOSE. Lesbian battering, or abuse, is a pattern of violent or coercive behaviours that one lesbian or bisexual woman uses to control the thoughts, beliefs, or conduct of her intimate same-sex partner or to punish her partner for resisting her attempts to control her. It can be physical, emotional, or sexual abuse, abuse related to your property, your money, threats, or homophobic control. I'm telling you this definition because often we think it can't be abuse unless there is physical abuse present. If you keep this definition in mind you'll be able to think of all the possible experiences a lesbian or bisexual woman may have in trying to access services. That's kind of a long definition: would you like anything clarified or repeated?

About services for lesbian abuse

5. If you had a lesbian or bisexual woman in an abusive same-sex relationship and she needed services and supports, what would be the first one you'd suggest to her? Can you think of other services and supports?

6. Thinking about this area of the province, what do you think your experience, or another lesbian or bisexual woman's experience, would be with trying to get help from a service organization if you or she was in an abusive relationship, either as an abuser or as abused.

7. Can you identify any gaps or barriers in access to services for women in abusive relationships that are different for lesbians or bisexual women?

In the next two questions we're wanting to find out if services need to be different for women who have been abused and women who are abusive.

8a. What do you think lesbians and other women in same-sex relationships who have been, or who are, abused need in the short term, i.e., in the first two weeks or so?

8b. What do you think these women need over the long term?

9a. What do you think lesbians or other women in same-sex relationships who have been, or who are, abusive need in the short term, i.e., the first two weeks or so?

9b. What do you think these women need over the long term?

10. How do you think being a lesbian or bisexual women who is even further marginalized—for example, who is Aboriginal or a woman of colour, who has a disability or is older, whose first language isn't English, who is young, or Jewish, or who has children—would affect her ability to use services for women in same-sex abusive relationships?

11. What do you think about the same organization providing services for lesbians and women in same-sex relationships who are abused and women who are abusive?

12a. Shelters and second-stage housing provide services for women in abusive relationships. These services vary a bit depending on the organization. What do you know about the services the shelter and second-stage house closest to you provides? What kind of reputation do they have?

12b. Have you heard anything about how this shelter/second-stage house treats lesbians and bisexual women, whether as staff, as volunteers, or as women seeking their services?

13. What do you think needs to be done in order for lesbians and other women in same-sex abusive relationships to receive services and support?

14. If you could create ideal services and supports for lesbians/women in same-sex relationships, including those in abusive relationships, what would those be, in whole or in part?

NB: Demographic information about participants and introductory remarks about the purpose of the project appeared on a separate page.

The above questions appear in appendixed material for the final report of the CLOSE Project (Balan, Chorney, and Ristock, 1995).

Appendix III

GUIDELINES FOR NEGOTIATING POWER PLAYS
IN LESBIAN RESEARCH

Identifying research questions

What are the more common research questions in your subject area? What assumptions are they based on? Whose interests do they serve? What risks are you able and willing to take?

Become aware of any political tensions that may surround your lesbian subject area. You may be able to anticipate some of the dynamics involved and the responses you may receive by talking with friends, members of affected communities, and colleagues.

Locating yourself

Why are you doing this research? What do you bring to this work? What roles and subject positions inform this work? How can you build self-reflexivity into the steps of the research?

Funding

Be prepared to be out or to find a way to do the work without funding. If you do apply for funding, be prepared to encounter homophobic opposition and to be visible as a lesbian.

Have allies, particularly allies who are members of the funding committees and who will be able to provide you with insider's knowledge.

Be unassailable in your application so that the lesbian topic is the only possible grounds for rejecting it—and if it is rejected, be prepared to complain about irregularities in the review procedure or discrimination on the basis of sexual orientation. Invoke your union contract if it offers any protection, and any other relevant human-rights documents.

What kind of funding sources have others turned to? What information do you have about the review process and committee members?

Sampling

Be prepared to be creative in your outreach efforts to overcome the obstacles of invisibility and fear of being out.

Since this invisibility makes most researchers of lesbian topics rely on snowball or purposive sampling, our research tends to be limited to the extended network of our own contacts. Design your research to move beyond your race and class limitations. Try to collect data from as diverse a group of respondents as possible.

Remember that not all of us identify with the term 'lesbian', and be aware of the terms preferred by the women you are trying to reach.

What are the obstacles to finding research participants? How can you move beyond some of these barriers? What language issues do you need to pay attention to in your outreach?

Confidentiality

Let participants know who you are and why you are doing the research. Their decision to participate will depend in part on your identifying yourself as lesbian and assuring them that you will respect their wishes for confidentiality and/or anonymity.

Remember how small lesbian communities are, and how easy it is to identify each other with minimal description. A lesbian researcher can be more threatening to the participant than a heterosexual researcher because she is more likely to come into contact with the participant's social network.

Consider safety issues for both researchers and participants, providing various levels of consent options and ensuring safe means of informing participants of your project and safe places to meet with participants.

Be mindful of researchers' and participants' individual differences in degrees and locales of outness.

How can you assure confidentiality? What safety issues do you have to be concerned with?

Accountability of the researcher

Consult with the communities affected by the research on your research design and objectives.

Think about the impact of the research on you, on research assistants, and on research participants. Provide opportunities for participants to process the impact of their involvement.

Also realize that because of the closet you may be the first person that the participant has confided in: be aware of her needs for a confidante and counsellor. Know who to refer her to.

Women often take personal risks to participate in your research. Try to give something back: contacts, resources, updates on the research, etc.

What are the ethical guidelines that inform your work with participants? What can you offer participants? What are they giving your? How can you build in reflexivity and accountability to the communities who are affected by your work?

Overall

Lesbian research in a homophobic society is by definition a political act. There is a real danger that results will be used to serve a homophobic agenda.

How can you use the research for constructive political action?

NB: These guidelines were developed with Catherine Taylor, who has been researching the emergence of lesbian studies in Canada.

Appendix IV

CONSENT FORMS:
PROGRAM EVALUATION OF 'CHOICES FOR YOUTH'

Information on the Evaluation

For: Young people in the program
From: Gale Burford, Jane Burnham, and Joan Pennell

Choices for Youth has hired us to perform an evaluation of the Program. During this early stage in planning the evaluation we want to meet you, let you know what we are up to, and look for your ideas about how this evaluation should be conducted. We are doing this because the CFY Program centres around involving youth in all decision-making in the agency, and because we strongly support this approach. You have every right to keep asking us questions until you have a clear understanding of what we are doing and why we are doing it. At the end of this meeting, we should understand each other's concerns and be very comfortable with the evaluation process. The following information is a way for us to introduce ourselves to you and to let you know what we hope to do.

By now you should be clear about why Choices for Youth is having an evaluation done and you should know and understand the aims of this evaluation. Our job is to do what is necessary to help CFY reach the aims of the evaluation. We plan to review the program and to gather the necessary information to determine how much the real program is like the plans for the program. We expect that staff, young people, and the Board of Directors will participate in the evaluation process and help us by giving us information we need. This meeting is one type of participation that we see as necessary to perform the kind of evaluation CFY wants.

To perform the evaluation, we will be gathering information relating to all parts of the program. This will include information on the principles or theoretical concepts used to guide decision-making at CFY; information on the current structure of the organization; information on staff, young people, and the board; information on services provided by the program and services the program connects with in the community; and information on financial provisions, facilities, equipment, and supplies.

In addition, we will be examining minutes from meetings, any policy or procedure manuals, and group and individual files. We will also interview staff, board members, young people, and people in the city whom CFY identifies as connected with this program. Some interviews will be group form, but most will be one-on-one interviews.

We plan to do this evaluation so that your right to privacy and confidentiality is respected. It is your choice whether to participate in the evaluation or not. However, please keep in mind that if everyone participates then we can give CFY an evaluation that is worth the money and the effort.

Attached is a **sample** consent form. If you choose to participate in the interviewing part of this evaluation you will be asked to sign such a form. Please read it carefully and if any part of the form is not clear, please tell us so we can explain what we mean and so we can change the wording so it is absolutely clear.

Consent to Participate in Program Evaluation and Research for Young People

I agree to participate in the Choices for Youth Program Evaluation Study being carried out by Dr Gale Burford and Dr Joan Pennell of Memorial University and Ms Jane Burnham who is a member of the evaluation team. I realize that I am under no obligation to participate, and I may withdraw from the study at any time without any problems.

I understand that:

1. The purpose of the evaluation is to find out how much Choices for Youth is doing compared to what it planned to do for the young people, to look at the strengths and weaknesses of the different programs, and to point out areas where change is needed.

2. My name will not be given in any verbal or written reports, or publications, made by the evaluators. The evaluators have assured me that they will do everything that they can to keep others from identifying me in the reports and publications.

3. I agree to be interviewed by myself or in a small group [circle and initial the type of interview]. The interview by myself will last about 1 to 1½ hours. The group interview will last about 1½ to 2 hours.

4. I agree to complete questionnaires relating to the program that the evaluators request. The questionnaires will take about 20 minutes to complete.

5. During the interview, I will be asked for my views about what works well at Choices for Youth and what could be improved. I will also be asked questions about my personal experiences with Choices for Youth.

6. I can refuse to answer any questions or leave the interview without having to explain, and my actions will not be reported to anyone.

7. At the end of the interview, I can read the notes and remove any of my comments, and up to two weeks after the interview, I can ask that information from my interview be taken out and not included in the evaluators' report.

8. Only the evaluators will read the interview notes. My name will not be written on the interview notes. I will be identified only by a number. The interview notes and the list of numbers for each name will be kept in separate locked cabinets which only the evaluators can open. The list of numbers for each name will be destroyed when the final report is accepted by Choices for Youth.

9. The evaluators will look at any written materials that the evaluators and the Choices for Youth Evaluation Committee agree are needed to do the evaluation. For example, these will include the minutes of all board meetings and board subcommittees, log recording, and group and individual files.

10. There is one situation where the evaluators will report information I give to them; that will happen:

    * if I am under the age of 16 and I reveal information to the evaluators about abuse of myself or any other young person who is under the age of 16, **and** if that abuse has not been previously reported, then the evaluators will report the information about that abuse to the Director of Child Welfare; **or**

    * if I am over the age of 16 and I reveal information to the evaluators that regards abuse of myself or any other young person over the age of 16 who is involved in Choices for Youth, **and**

    * if the abuse is committed by someone in Choices for Youth, then the information about that abuse will be reported to two members of the Board of Directors of Choices for Youth not named in the abuse.

11. If you provide information that indicates you are going to cause immediate and serious physical harm to yourself or to any other person the information will be passed on to your counsellors.

12. This consent form will be stored in a separate place from any other materials used in the evaluation, and it will be destroyed once the final report is accepted by Choices for Youth.

I have read this consent form and understand what it says. I am participating freely without any promises of benefits from the evaluators. I acknowledge that I have been offered a copy of this form. The Interviewer's Guidelines for Informed Consent have been read to me.

My signature is my consent to participate in the interview and to give the evaluators access to information as specified in this consent form.

Signature of Participant   Date

I, the undersigned, have, to the best of my ability, fully explained the nature of this evaluation study. I have invited questions and provided answers. I believe that the person whose signature appears above understands the implications and voluntary nature of their involvement in this evaluation study.

Signature of Evaluator   Date

Interviewer's Guidelines for Informed Consent

1. *Purpose of the study:*
Choices for Youth has hired Gale Burford, Joan Pennell, and Jane Burnham to do an evaluation of the program to help us find out what has happened in the program compared to what was planned for the program, and to help us decide what changes or improvements can be made. The evaluators' job is to follow a plan to help Choices for Youth reach the aim we set for the evaluation. Choices for Youth representatives will agree with each step of this plan before the evaluators begin that step.

2. *Description of the procedure:*
Interviews: To carry out the evaluation the evaluators plan to interview young people, staff, and board members for their views of the program. The evaluators plan to interview those who are with the program now and those who have left the program. They plan to interview people outside Choices for Youth, but who have been involved enough to offer useful information. Some interviews will be individual and some will be small-group. [record which type of interview the individual chooses] The individual interviews will last for about 1 to 1½ hours each and the group interviews will last about 1½ to 2 hours each.
Questionnaires: The evaluators would like young people and staff to complete questionnaires about the program. The questionnaires take about 20 minutes to complete.

Document review: The evaluators plan to read all materials that Choices for Youth representatives agree are needed for the evaluation. The material they plan to read will pertain to the program, the lives of the young people and the organization as a whole. The material will include board meeting and committee minutes, logs, and files.

Visits: In addition, the evaluators would like to visit each of the facilities and speak to people who live and work there.

3. *Duration of the evaluation:*
The evaluation proposal was accepted on February 21, 1992 and will be completed by the end of May, 1992.

4. *Risks, discomforts, inconveniences:*
The evaluators will try not to get in the way of the organization or people involved with the program while they carry out the evaluation. The evaluators have set up meetings with the CFY Evaluation Committee to try and keep up with people's feelings during the evaluation. We want you to tell members of this group if you feel frustrated or if you feel pleased with the evaluation. You do not have to take part in the evaluation. If you take part in an interview, you can refuse to answer any questions or you can leave an interview without having to explain and you will not be reported to anyone. You can decide whether or not you want your individual file to be read by the evaluators. No names or identifying information will be in copies of individual files which the evaluators read and their notes will identify you by a number, not a name. In their reports, the evaluators will do everything they can to keep others from identifying you.

5. *Benefits which participants in the study might receive:*
There are no immediate or direct benefits to you for taking part in this evaluation. Nevertheless, the results and recommendations of the evaluation may turn out to be useful for improving the services offered through CFY; however, this will depend on how the recommendations are used by Choices for Youth.

6. *Confidentiality:*
Any and all information which you share in the interview and which the evaluators read in the files will be held confidential. The only exception will be reports made to the evaluators about verbal, physical, or sexual abuse of a young person. If you tell the evaluators of an abuse situation, you must know that they will report the information to protect the young people. Every attempt will be made to keep your identity confidential; however, if you report abuse, others may realize that you provided the information. All other

information will remain confidential. Under no other circumstances will the evaluators connect your name with the information you give to them about the program or with personal information you tell them about yourself.

7. *Dissemination of information:*
All reports and publications which use information from the evaluation will present the information so that no individual in the program can be identified.

Consent to Allow Access to Personal Files for Program Evauluation and Research [for Young People]

I agree to allow either Dr Gale Burford, Dr Joan Pennell, or Ms Jane Burnham, who are members of the evaluation team performing an evaluation of the Choices for Youth Program, to look at any and all files about me and which are maintained by Choices for Youth. I realize that I am under no obligation to grant consent to any files on me.

I understand that:

1. The purpose of allowing the evaluators to review my personal files is to help them find out how much Choices for Youth is doing for young people compared to how much it planned to do. This information will help the evaluators identify parts of the program which could be improved by change.

2. The evaluators can only read my personal files after all information which might identify me, or information I do not want read by the evaluators, has been removed either by me or, with my permission, by my counsellor.

3. Copies of my file, which have had identifying information removed,will only be read by the evaluators and will be read in the offices of Choices for Youth. The evaluators will only be permitted to remove their notes on the files from the office. The evaluators' notes will not contain names or any other identifying information.

4. Notes that the evaluators make on personal files will be kept in a locked cabinet until two months after the evaluators' report has been accepted and approved. At that time the notes will be destroyed.

5. The evaluators have assured me that my identity will not be revealed in any verbal or written reports, or publications by them.

6. Once I have signed this consent form and the identifying information has been removed from my file, the form and the copy of my file will be held for one week by a counsellor with CFY. During this week, I can change my mind and withdraw my consent to have any file read by the evaluators.

7. Once the evaluators have looked at my files, I cannot ask to have any information that came from my files removed from the evaluators' report.

8. This consent form will be stored in a locked cabinet and it will be destroyed once the final report is accepted by Choices for Youth.

I have read this consent form and understand what it says. I am participating freely without any promises of benefits from the evaluators. I acknowledge that I have been offered a copy of this form. The Interviewer's Guidelines for Informed Consent have been read to me.

My signature is my consent to give the evaluators access to information as specified in this consent form.

Signature of Participant   Date

I, the undersigned, have, to the best of my ability, fully explained the nature of this evaluation study. I have invited questions and provided answers. I believe that the person whose signature appears above understands the implications and voluntary nature of their allowing the evaluators access to personal files.

Signature of Staff Member   Date

References

Acker, Joan, Kate Barry, and Joke Esseveld. (1983). Objectivity and truth: Problems in doing feminist research. *Women's Studies International Forum*, 6 (4), 423–35.

Alary, Jacques, Marie-Chantal Guédon, Claude Larivière, and Robert Mazer (Eds). (1990). *Community care and participatory research* (Susan Usher, Trans.). Montréal: Nu-Age Editions.

Alcoff, Linda. (1991). The problem of speaking for others. *Cultural Critique*, 20, 5–32.

Alcoff, Linda, and Laura Gray. (1993). Survivor discourse: Transgression or recuperation? *Signs: Journal of Women in Culture and Society*, 18 (2), 260–90.

Anderson, Joan. (1991). Reflexivity in fieldwork: Toward a feminist epistemology. *IMAGE: Journal of Nursing Scholarship*, 23 (2), 115–18.

Armitage, Andrew. (1993). Family and child welfare in the First Nation communities. In Wharf (1993), 131–71.

Balan, Angie, Rhonda Chorney, and Janice L. Ristock. (1995). *Training and educatio: project for responding to abuse in lesbian relationships.* Winnipeg, Man.: Family Violence Prevention Division, Health Canada.

Barber, Benjamin. (1984). *Strong democracy: Participatory politics for a new age.* Berkeley: University of California.

Barley, Stephan R. (1991). Semiotics and the study of occupational and organizational culture. In Frost et al. (1991), 39–54.

Barnsley, Jan, and Diana Ellis. (1987). *Action research for women's groups.* Vancouver, BC: Women's Research Centre.

Bear, Shirley, with Tobique Women's Group. (1991). 'You can't change the Indian Act?'. In Wine and Ristock (1991), 198–220.

Benton-Benai, Edward. (1988). *The Mishomis book: The voice of the Ojibway.* St Paul, Minn: Red School House.

Benveniste, Emile. (1971). *Problems in general linguistics.* (Mary E. Meek, Trans.). Coral Gables, Fla: University of Miami Press.

Bhavnani, Kum-Kum. (1994). Tracing the contours: Feminist research and feminist objectivity. In Haleh Afshar and Mary Maynard (Eds). *The dynamics of 'race' and gender: Some feminist interventions*, 26–40. London: Taylor and Francis.

Briskin, Linda. (1991). Feminist practice: A new approach to evaluating feminist strategy. In Wine and Ristock (1991), 24–40.

Brown, Laura. (1989). New voices, new visions: Toward a lesbian/gay paradigm for psychology. *Psychology of Women Quarterly*, 13 (4), 445–58.

Brown, Lyn M., and Carol Gilligan. (1992). *Meeting at the crossroads: Women's psychology and girls' development.* Cambridge, Mass.: Harvard University Press.

Buffalo, Yvonne R.D. (1990). Seeds of thought, arrows of change: Native story-telling as metaphor. In Toni A. Laidlaw, Cheryl Malmo, and Associates (Eds). *Healing voices: Feminist approaches to therapy with women*, 118–42. San Francisco: Jossey-Bass.

Burford, Gale, Joan Pennell, and Jane Burnham. (1992). *Having a say: From phasing out Mt. Cashel to a model of community living for young adults*. St John's, Nfld: Program Evaluation of Choices for Youth.

Burford, Gale, and Michelle Sullivan. (1990). *Diagnosis of an ailing system of services: Post-mortem on the Coach House*. St John's, Nfld: Department of Social Services, Division of Child Welfare, Funded Program Evaluation.

Burman, Erica. (1992). Feminism and discourse in developmental psychology: Power, subjectivity and interpretation. *Feminism & Psychology*, 2 (1), 45–59.

Burman, Erica, and Ian Parker (Eds). (1993). *Discourse analytic research. Repertoires and readings of text in action*. London: Routledge.

Butler, Judith. (1991). Imitation and gender subordination. In Diana Fuss, Ed. (1991). *Inside out: Lesbian theories, gay theories*, 13–31. New York: Routledge.

Callahan, Marilyn. (1993). Feminist approaches: Women recreate child welfare. In Wharf (1993), 172–209.

Canadian Panel on Violence Against Women. (1993). *Changing the landscape*. Ottawa: Minister of Supply and Services.

Charter, Ann. (1993). A medicine wheel approach to working with men who batter. Unpublished manuscript. Faculty of Social Work, University of Manitoba, Winnipeg.

Chesley, Laurie, Donna MacAulay, and Janice L. Ristock. (1991). *Abuse in lesbian relationships: A handbook of information and resources*. Toronto: Toronto Counselling Centre for Lesbians and Gays.

Culler, Jonathan. (1982). *On deconstruction: Theory and criticism after structuralism*. Ithaca, NY: Cornell University Press.

Dallmayr, Fred R., and Thomas A. McCarthy. (Eds). (1977). *Understanding and social inquiry*. Notre Dame, Ind.: Notre Dame Press.

Dankwort, Jürgen. (1988). The challenge of accountability in treating wife abusers: A critique from Québec. *Canadian Journal of Community Health*, 7 (2), 103–17.

Debo, Angie. (1970). *A history of the Indians of the United States*. Norman: University of Oklahoma Press.

de Lauretis, Teresa. (1987). *Technologies of gender: Essays on theory, film, and fiction*. Indianapolis: Indiana University Press.

Denzin, Norman K. (1989). *The research act: A theoretical introduction to sociological methods* (3rd ed.). Englewood Cliffs, NJ: Prentice Hall.

Derrida, Jacques. (1981). *Positions* (Alan Bass, Trans.). Chicago: University of Chicago Press. (Original work published 1972).

———. (1982). *Margins of philosophy.* (Alan Bass, Trans.). Chicago: University of Chicago Press. (Original work published 1972).

Devaux, Monique. (1994). Feminism and empowerment: A critical reading of Foucault. *Feminist Studies,* 20, 223–48.

Drover, Glenn, and Patrick Kerans (Eds). (1993). *New approaches to welfare theory.* Aldershot, Harts.: Edward Elgar.

Dufrene, Phoebe. (1990). Utilizing the arts for healing from a native American perspective: Implications for creative arts therapies. *Canadian Journal of Native Studies,* 10 (1), 121–31.

Faludi, Susan. (1995). 'I'm not a feminist but I play one on TV'. *Ms,* March/April, 31–9.

Fekete, John. (1994). *Moral panic: Biopolitics rising.* Montreal: Robert Davis.

Fine, Michelle. (1992). *Disruptive voices: The possibilities of feminist research.* Ann Arbor: University of Michigan Press.

Fine, Michelle, and Jaquie Wade. (1986). *Evaluation of domestic violence programs in Tennessee.* San Francisco: Hilton Foundation.

Fonow, Mary M., and Judith A. Cook (Eds). (1991). *Beyond methodology: Feminist scholarship as lived research.* Bloomington: Indiana University Press.

Foucault, Michel. (1977). *Discipline and punish: The birth of the prison* (A. Sheridan, Trans.) London: Allen Lane.

Freire, Paulo. (1970). *Pedagogy of the oppressed.* New York: Continuum.

Friedmann, John. (1987). *Planning in the public domain: From knowledge to action.* Princeton, NJ: Princeton University Press.

Frost, Peter J., Larry F. Moore, Meryl R. Louis, Craig C. Lundberg, and Joanne Martin (Eds). (1991). *Reframing organizational culture.* Newbury Park, Cal.: Sage.

Galloway, David. (1994). The role of consultants in reviewing provision for special educational needs: Cautionary tales. *Evaluation and Research in Education,* 8 (1 & 2), 97–107.

Gavey, Nicola. (1989). Feminist poststructuralism and discourse analysis: Contributions to feminist psychology. *Psychology of Women Quarterly,* 13, 459–75.

Geertz, Clifford. (1983). *Local knowledge: Further essays in interpretive anthropology.* New York: Basic Books.

———. (1984). Anti anti-relativism. *American Anthropologist,* 86 (2), 263–78.

Gelles, Richard J., and Donileen Loeske. (1993). *Current controversies on family violence.* Newbury Park, Cal.: Sage.

Gilman, Susan T. (1988). A history of the sheltering movement for battered women in Canada. *Canadian Journal of Community Mental Health*, 7 (2), 9–21.

Giroux, Henry A. (1991). Introduction: Modernism, postmodernism, and feminism: Rethinking the boundaries of educational discourse. In Henry A. Giroux (Ed.). *Postmodernism, feminism, and cultural politics: Redrawing educational boundaries*, 1–59. Albany: State University of New York Press.

Glaser, Barney G., and Anselm L. Strauss. (1967). *The discovery of grounded theory: Strategies for qualitative research*. New York: Aldine.

Goodman, Lisa A., Mary P. Koss, Louise F. Fitzgerald, Nancy Felipe-Russo, and Gwendolyn Puryear Keita. (1993). Male violence against women: Current research and future directions. *The American Psychologist*, 48, 1054–8.

Gordon, Linda. (1988). *Heroes in their own lives: The politics and history of family violence*. New York: Viking.

Gorman, Jane. (1993). Postmodernism and the conduct of inquiry in social work. *AFFILIA: Journal of Women and Social Work*, 8 (3), 247–64.

Gouldner, Alvin. (1971). *The coming crisis in western sociology*. London: Heinemann Educational Books.

Greaves, Lorraine, Alison Wylie, and the Staff of the Battered Women's Advocacy Centre. (1995). Women and violence: Feminist practice and quantitative method. In Sandra Burt and Lorraine Code (Eds). *Changing methods: Feminists transforming practice*. Peterborough, Ont.: Broadview Press.

Greimas, Algirdas J. (1983). *Structural semantics: An attempt at a method*. (Daniele McDowell, Ronald Schleifer, and Alan Velie, Trans.) Lincoln: University of Nebraska Press.

———. (1987). *On meaning: Selected writings in semiotic theory*. (Paul J. Perron and Frank H. Collins, Trans.). Minneapolis: University of Minnesota Press. (Original works published 1970, 1976, 1983).

———. (1990). *The social sciences: A semiotic view*. (Paul Perron and Frank H. Collins, Trans.). Minneapolis: University of Minnesota Press.

Hammersley, Martyn E. (1989). *The dilemma of quantitative method: Herbert Blumer and the Chicago tradition*. London: Routledge.

Hammersley, Martyn E., and Paul Atkinson. (1983). *Ethnography: Principles and practice*. London: Tavistock.

Harding, Sandra. (1986). *The science question in feminism*. Ithaca: Cornell University Press.

——— (Ed.). (1987). *Feminism and methodology: Social science issues*. Bloomington: Indiana University Press.

Harvey, Irene E. (1986). *Derrida and the economy of difference*. Bloomington: Indiana University Press.

Herek, Gregory M., and Kevin T. Berrill (Eds). (1992). *Hate crimes: Confronting violence against lesbians and gay men.* Newbury Park, Cal.: Sage.

Herman, J. (1992). *Trauma and recovery: The aftermath of violence from domestic abuse and political terror.* New York: Basic Books.

Herman, Joan L., Lynn L. Morris, and Carol T. Fitz-Gibbon. (1987). *Evaluator's handbook.* Newbury Park, Cal.: Sage.

Hoare, Tony, Chris Levy, and Michael P. Robinson. (1993). Participatory action research in Native communities: Cultural opportunities and legal implications. *Canadian Journal of Native Studies,* 13 (1), 43–68.

Hoehne, Dieter. (1988). Self-help and social change. In Frank Cunningham, Sue Findlay, Marlene Kadar, Alan Lennon, and Ed Silva (Eds). *Social movements/social change: The politics and practice of organizing,* 236–51. Toronto: Between the Lines.

hooks, bell. (1990). *Yearning: Race, gender, and cultural politics.* Toronto: Between the Lines.

Hughes, Samuel H.S. (1991). *Royal Commission of Inquiry into the response of the Newfoundland criminal justice system to complaints.* St John's, Nfld: Queen's Printer.

Hyde, Cheryl. (1994). Reflections on a journey: A research story. In Catherine K. Riessman (Ed.). *Qualitative studies in social work research,* 169–89. Thousand Oaks, Cal.: Sage.

Ihde, Don. (1971). *Hermeneutic phenomenology: The philosophy of Paul Ricoeur.* Evanston, Ill.: Northwestern University Press.

Jameson, Fredric. (1972). *The prison-house of language: A critical account of structuralism and Russian formalism.* Princeton, NJ: Princeton University Press.

Kelly, L. (1988). *Surviving sexual violence.* Minneapolis: University of Minnesota Press.

Kérisit, Michèle, and Nérée St-Amand. (1994). Taking risks with families at risk: Some alternative approaches with poor families in Canada. In Joe Hudson and Burt Galaway (Eds). *Child welfare in Canada: Research and policy implications,* 154–67. Toronto: Thompson Educational Publishing.

Kirby, Sandra, and Kate McKenna. (1989). *Experience, research, social change: Methods from the margins.* Toronto: Garamond Press.

Kitzinger, Celia. (1987). *The social construction of lesbianism.* London: Sage.

———. (1991). Feminism, psychology and the paradox of power. *Feminism and Psychology,* 1, 111–29.

Klein, Renate. (1986). The dynamics of Women's Studies: Its international ideas and practices in higher education. Doctoral dissertation: Institute of Education, University of London.

Koss, Mary P. (1990). The women's health research agenda: Violence against women. *American Psychologist,* 45, 374–80.

Koss, Mary P., Lisa A. Goodman, Angela Browne, Louise F. Fitzgerald, Gwendolyn Puryear Keita, and Nancy Felipe Russo. (1994). *No safe haven: Male violence against women at home, at work, and in the community.* Washington, DC: American Psychological Association.

Krippendorff, Klaus. (1980). *Content analysis: An introduction to its methodology.* Beverly Hills, Cal.: Sage.

Kritzman, Lawrence D. (Ed.). (1988). *Politics, philosophy, culture: Interviews and other writings of Michel Foucault,* 1977–1984. New York: Routledge.

Laframboise, Donna. (1996). *The princess at the window: A new gender morality.* Toronto: Penguin.

Lane, Phil. (1984). *The Sacred Tree.* Lethbridge, Alta: Four Worlds Development Project.

Lather, Patti. (1986). Research as praxis. *Harvard Educational Review,* 56 (3), 257–77.

———. (1991). *Getting smart: Feminist research and pedagogy with/in the postmodern.* New York: Routledge.

———. (1992). Critical frames in educational research: Feminist and post-structural perspectives. *Theory into Practice,* 31 (2), 87–99.

Lee, Raymond M., and Claire M. Renzetti. (1990). The problems of researching sensitive topics: An overview and introduction. *American Behavioral Scientist,* 33 (5), 510–28.

Lenskyj, Helen. (1990). The treatment of the sexualities in research. *Resources for Feminist Research,* 19, 91–4.

Little Bear, Leroy. (1986). Aboriginal rights and the Canadian 'grundnorm'. In J. Rick Ponting (Ed.). *Arduous journey: Canadian Indians and decolonization,* 243–59. Toronto: McClelland and Stewart.

Lorde, Audre. (1984). *Sister outsider: Essays and speeches.* Freedom, Cal.: Crossing Press.

Lynch, Barry, Diane Molloy, Michelle Sullivan, Tim Turner, and representatives of Mount Cashel residents. (1991). Unfinished business: The Mount Cashel experience. *Journal of Child and Youth Care,* 6 (1), 55–66.

Lyons, Oren. (1984). Spirituality, equality, and natural law. In Leroy Little Bear, Menno Boldt, and J. Anthony Long (Eds). *Pathways to self-determination: Canadian Indians and the Canadian state,* 5–13. Toronto: University of Toronto Press.

Lyotard, J.F. (1984). *The postmodern condition: A report on knowledge.* Manchester: Manchester University Press.

Ma Mawi Wi Chi Itata Centre, Inc. (1993). *Family violence program model.* Ottawa: Health and Welfare Canada, Health and Social Programs Branch.

McDermott, Kathleen. (1987). In and out of the game: A case study of contract research. In G. Clare Wenger (Ed.). *The research relationship: Practice and politics in social policy research*. London: Allen and Unwin.

McDonald, Barry. (1993). A political classification of evaluation studies in education. In M. Hammersley (Ed.). *Social research: Philosophy, politics and practice*, 105–8. London: Sage.

MacLeod, Linda. (1987). *Battered but not beaten . . . : Preventing wife battering in Canada*. Ottawa: Canadian Advisory Council on the Status of Women.

McRobbie, Angela. (1993). Feminism, postmodernism and the real me. *Theory, Culture & Society*, 10, 127–42.

Maguire, Patricia. (1987). *Doing participatory research: A feminist approach*. Amherst: Center for International Education, School of Education, University of Massachusetts.

Mansbridge, Jane J. (1983). *Beyond adversary democracy*. New York: Basic Books.

Martindale, Kathleen. (1994). Power, ethics, and polyvocal feminist theory. In Barbara Godard (Ed.). *Collaboration in the feminine: Writings on women and culture from Tessera*. Toronto: Second Story Press.

Mertens, Donna M., Joanne Farley, Anna-Marie Madison, and Patti Singleton. (1994). Diverse voices in evaluation practice: Feminists, minorities, and persons with disabilities. *Evaluation Practice*, 15 (2), 123–38.

Mies, Maria, Veronika Bennholdt-Thomsen, and Claudia Werlhof. (1988). *Women: The last colony*. London: Zed Books.

Miles, Angela. (1991). Reflections on integrative feminism and rural women. In Wine and Ristock (1991), 56–74.

Morawski, Jill G. (1994). *Practicing feminisms, reconstructing psychology: Notes on a liminal science*. Ann Arbor: University of Michigan Press.

Morgen, Sandra. (1983). Towards a politics of 'feelings': Beyond the dialectic of thought and action. *Women's Studies*, 10, 203–23.

———. (1994). Personalizing personnel decisions in feminist organizational theory and practice. *Human Relations*, 6, 665–84.

National Coalition against Domestic Violence. (1995). *Voice*, special editions: *Issues that divide us* (1993); *Anti-homophobia* (Spring 1991); *Women of colour in the movement* (Fall 1989).

Oakley, Ann. (1981). Interviewing women: A contradiction in terms. In Helen Roberts (Ed.). *Doing feminist research*, 30–61. London: Routledge and Kegan Paul.

O'Kelly, C., and L. Carney. (1986). *Women and men in society: Cross cultural perspectives on gender stratification*. Belmont, Cal.: Wadsworth.

Opie, Annie. (1992). Qualitative research, appropriation of the 'other' and empowerment. *Feminist Review*, 40, 52–69.

Ott, J. Steven. (1989). *The organizational culture perspective*. Pacific Grove, Cal.: Brooks/Cole Publishing.

Paglia, Camilla. (1992). *Sex, art and American culture*. New York: Vintage.

Parker, Ian. (1992). *Discourse dynamics: Critical analysis for social and individual psychology*. London: Routledge.

Parlett, R., and M. Hamilton. (1977). *Introduction to illuminative evaluation: Studies in higher education*. Cardiff-by-the-Sea, Cal.: Pacific Sounding Press.

Patte, Daniel. (1990). *The religious dimensions of Biblical texts: Greimas's structural semiotics and Biblical exegesis*. Atlanta, Ga: Scholars Press.

Patton, Michael Q. (1990). *Qualitative evaluation and research methods* (2nd ed.). Newbury Park, Cal.: Sage.

Pearson, Sue. (1994). *An overview of poverty related research projects supported by National Welfare Grants*. Ottawa: National Welfare Grants, Human Resource Development Canada.

Pennell, Joan. (1987). Ideology at a Canadian shelter for battered women: A reconstruction. *Women's Studies International Forum*, 10 (2), 113–23.

———. (1990a). Consensual bargaining: Labor negotiations in battered-women's programs. *Journal of Progressive Human Services*, 1 (1), 59–74.

———. (1990b). Democratic hierarchy in feminist organizations. In *Dissertation Abstracts International*, 50(1-A). (University Microfilms No. AAD90-15034).

———. (1990c). Knitting empowering configurations. In Joan Turner (Ed.). *Living the changes*, 188–96. Winnipeg: University of Manitoba.

———. (1991). The participation of non-native workers in aboriginal social services. Paper presented at the panel 'Aboriginal community services on family violence', at the conference Alternatives: Directions in the Nineties to End Abuse of Women, Winnipeg, Man.

———. (1992). *Images of labour unionized shelters for abused women: Initial report*. Memorial University of Newfoundland: School of Social Work (available in English or French).

———. (1993). Should shelter staff unionize? *Perception*, 17 (3), 25–7.

———. (1995). Feminism and labour unions: Transforming state regulation of women's programs. *Journal of Progressive Human Services*, 6 (1).

Joan Pennell and Gale Burford. (1993). Young people having a say: *An alternative community within the social welfare system*. Paper presented at the panel 'Reforms and Innovation in Child Welfare', at the 6th Biennial Social Welfare Policy Conference, Rethinking Social Welfare: People, Policy and Practice, St John's, Nfld.

———. (1994). Widening the circle: The family group decision making project. *Journal of Child & Youth Care* 9 (1), 1–12.

Joan Pennell, Maureen Flaherty, Naomi Gravel, Eveline Milliken, and Mallory Neuman. (1993). Feminist social work education in mainstream and nonmainstream classrooms. *AFFILIA: Journal of Women and Social Work*, 8(3), 317–38.

Phelan, Shane. (1993). (Be)Coming out: Lesbian identity and politics. *Signs: Journal of Women in Culture and Society*, 18 (4), 765–90.

Potucheck, Jean L. (1986). The context of social service funding: The funding relationship. *Social Service Review*, 60, 421–36.

Rappaport, Julian. (1990). Research methods and the empowerment social agenda. In Tolan et al. (1990), 51–63.

Reinelt, Claire. (1994). Fostering empowerment, building community: The challenges for state-funded feminist organizations. *Human Relations*, 6, 685–705.

Reinharz, Shulamit. (1992). *Feminist methods in social research*. New York: Oxford.

———. (1993). Neglected voices and excessive demands in feminist research. *Qualitative Sociology*, 1, 69–76.

Renzetti, Claire M. (1992). *Violent betrayal*. Newbury Park, Cal.: Sage.

Richan, Willard. (1992). The alternative agency as an active learner: A case study. *Journal of the National Association of Social Workers*, 37 (5), 406–11.

Ricoeur, Paul. (1981). *Hermeneutics and the human sciences: Essays on language, action and interpretation.* (John B. Thompson, Ed. and Trans.). Cambridge: Cambridge University Press.

Riger, Stephanie. (1984). On being on their side. *The Division of Community Psychology of the American Psychological Association Bulletin*, Summer.

———. (1989). The politics of community intervention. *American Journal of Community Psychology*, 17 (3), 379–83.

———. (1990). Ways of knowing and organizational approaches to community research. In Tolan et al. (1990), 42–50.

———. (1993). What's wrong with empowerment. *American Journal of Community Psychology*, 21 (3), 279–92.

———. (1994). Challenges of success: Stages of growth in feminist organizations. *Feminist Studies*, 20 (2), 275–300.

Ristock, Janice L. (1987). Working together for empowerment: Feminist social service collectives in Canada. *Canadian Woman Studies*, 8 (4), 74–6.

———. (1989). Feminist social service collectives in Canada—A viable force or a contradiction. Doctoral dissertation, University of Toronto.

———. (1990). Canadian feminist social service agencies: Caring and contradictions. In Lisa Albrecht and Rose Brewer (Eds). *Bridges of power: Women's multicultural alliances*, 172–81. Philadelphia: New Society.

———. (1991a). Beyond ideologies: Understanding abuse in lesbian relationships. *Canadian Woman Studies*, 12 (1), 74–9.

———. (1991b). Feminist collectives: The struggles and contradictions in our quest for a uniquely feminist structure. In Wine and Ristock (1991), 41–55.

———. (1993). The theory and politics of helping in feminist social service collectives. In Drover and Kerans (1993), 220–31.

———. (1994). 'And justice for all?' . . . The social context of legal responses to abuse in lesbian relationships. *Canadian Journal of Women and the Law*, 7 (2), 415–30.

———. (forthcoming). Kiss and kill: Some impacts of cultural representations of women's sexualities. In Pauline Greenhill and Diane Tye (Eds). *The (dis)place(ment) of female traditional culture in Canada.*

Rockhill, Kathleen. (1987). The chaos of subjectivity in the ordered halls of academe. *Canadian Woman Studies*, 8 (4), 12–17.

Rodriguez, Noelie M. (1988). A successful feminist shelter: A case study of the family crisis shelter in Hawaii. *Journal of Applied Behavioral Science*, 24 (30), 235–50.

Roiphe, Katie. (1993). *The morning after: Sex, fear and feminism*. Boston: Little Brown.

Rothschild, Joyce, and J. Allen Whitt. (1986). *The cooperative workplace: Potentials and dilemmas of organizational democracy and participation*. Cambridge: Cambridge University Press.

Said, Edward. (1989). Representing the colonized: Anthropology's interlocutors. *Critical Inquiry*, 15, 205–25.

Schein, E. (1987). *Organizational culture and leadership*. San Francisco: Jossey-Bass.

Schleifer, Ronald. (1987). *A.J. Greimas and the nature of meaning: Linguistics, semiotics and discourse theory.* Lincoln: University of Nebraska Press.

Seymour, Phyllis, and Cheryl Hebert. (1991). *Mount Cashel orphanage: Phase-out project final report*. St John's: Government of Newfoundland and Labrador, Department of Social Services.

Smith, Dorothy. (1990). *The conceptual practices of power: A feminist sociology of knowledge*. Boston: Northeastern University Press.

Sommers, Christina Hoff. (1994). *Who stole feminism? How women have betrayed women*. New York: Simon and Schuster.

Spivak, Gayatri Chakrovorty. (1987). *In other worlds: Essays in cultural politics*. New York: Methuen.

Srinivasan, Meera, and Liane V. Davis. (1991). A shelter: An organization like any other? *AFFILIA: Journal of Women and Social Work*, 6 (1), 38–57.

Stanley, Liz. (Ed.). (1990). *Feminist praxis*. London: Routledge.

———. (1993). On auto/biography in sociology. *Sociology, 27* (1), 41–52.

Stanley, Liz, and Sue Wise. (1993). *Breaking out again: Feminist ontology and epistemology*. London: Routledge.

Stivers, Camilla. (1993). Reflections on the role of personal narrative in social science. *Signs: Journal of Women in Culture and Society,* 18 (2), 408–25.

Storm, Hyemeyohsts. (1972). *Seven arrows*. New York: Harper and Row.

Strauss, Anselm L., and Juliet Corbin. (1990). *Basics of qualitative research: Grounded theory procedures and techniques*. Newbury Park, Cal.: Sage.

Stull, David D., and Jean J. Schensul (Eds). (1987). *Collaborative research and social change: Applied anthropology in action*. Boulder, Colo.: Westview Press.

Sullivan, Michelle, Rob Fildes, and Tim Turner. (1993). The wheel of fortune: An analysis of factors influencing the development and growth of not-for-profit child and youth care options in the province of Newfoundland and Labrador. Paper presented at the sixth Biennial Social Welfare Policy Conference, St John's, Nfld.

Swift, Karen. (1991). Contradictions in child welfare: Neglect and responsibility. In Carol T. Baines, Patricia M. Evans, and Sheila M. Neysmith (Eds). *Women's caring: Feminist perspectives on social welfare,* 234–71. Toronto: McClelland and Stewart.

Swigonski, Mary E. (1993). Feminist standpoint theory and the questions of social work research. *AFFILIA: Journal of Women and Social Work,* 8 (2), 171–83.

Taylor, Sharon. (1992). Gender in development: A feminist process for transforming university and society. In P. Sachdev, G. Burford, L. Cregheur, R. Ommer, J. Pennell, and W. Rowe (Eds). *Oval works: Feminist social work scholarship,* 25–40. Memorial University of Newfoundland: School of Social Work.

———. (1994). Communicating for empowerment: Women's initiatives to overcome poverty in rural Thailand and Newfoundland. In Pilar Riano (Ed.). *Women in grassroots communication: Furthering social change,* 235–50. Newbury Park, Cal.: Sage.

Taylor, Sharon, and Cathy Forristall, Pat Power, Trudy Ryan, Gale Burford, Janice Parsons, and Joan Pennell. (1995). *Standing strong: Single mothers' overcoming barriers to post-secondary education*. Final report of the Hoops and Hurdles Research Project to Human Resources Development Canada, National Welfare Grants, Ottawa.

Tolan, Patrick, Christopher Keys, Fern Chertok, and Leonard Jason (Eds). (1990). *Researching community psychology: Issues of theory and methods*. Washington, DC: American Psychological Association.

Vicker, Jill. (1991). Bending the iron law of oligarchy: Debates on the feminization of organization and political process in the English Canadian women's movement, 1970-1988. In Wine and Ristock (1991), 75–94.

Walker, Gillian A. (1990). *Family violence and the women's movement: The conceptual politics of struggle.* Toronto: University of Toronto Press.

Walkerdine, Valerie. (1981). Sex, power and pedagogy. *Screen Education*, 38, 14–24.

———. (1990). *Schoolgirl fictions.* London: Verso.

Wasserfall, Rachel. (1993). Reflexivity, feminism and difference. *Qualitative Sociology*, 16 (1), 23–41.

Wharf, Brian. (Ed.). (1993). *Rethinking child welfare in Canada.* Toronto: McClelland and Stewart.

Whyte, William F. (Ed.). (1991). *Participatory action research*. Newbury Park, Cal.: Sage.

Wine, Jeri D., and Janice L. Ristock (Eds). (1991). *Women and social change: Feminist activism in Canada.* Toronto: James Lorimer.

Witten, Marsha. (1993). Narrative and the culture of obedience at the workplace. In Dennis K. Mumby (Ed.). *Narrative and social control: Critical perspectives.* London: Sage.

Women's Research Centre (Diana Ellis, Gayla Reid, and Jan Barnsley). (1990). *Keeping on track: An evaluation guide for community groups.* Vancouver: Women's Research Centre.

Young, Iris Marion. (1990). The ideal of community and the politics of difference. In Linda J. Nicholson (Ed.). *Feminism/Postmodernism*, 300–23. New York: Routledge.

———. (1994). Punishment, treatment, empowerment: Three approaches to policy for pregnant addicts. *Feminist Studies*, 20 (1), 33–57.

Yuval-Davis, Nira. (1994). Women, ethnicity and empowerment. *Feminism & Psychology*, 4 (1), 179–97.

Index

Laframboise, Donna, 100
Language, 74; and power, 6, 9–10, 100; *see also* Discourse; Discursive conditions
Lather, Patti, 1, 16, 50
Lesbian research, 15, 57–63; data analysis, 76; ethical issues, 75–6, 129; finding participants, 74; funding, 73–4 guidelines, 128–30; methodological issues, 72–7
Linguistics, structural, 85; *see also* Structuralism, linguistic
Links, feminist, x, 1, 3, 8, 9, 80, 81, 83; 'links and interruptions' methodology, x, 9, 10–11, 13, 14, 35, 79, 97, 113; *see also* Interruptions
Location, researcher's, 11, 12, 13, 65–6, 67, 68, 69–70, 76, 115, 128; in organizational consulting, 37, 38, 39, 41, 43; *see also* Identity; Subjectivity
Lorde, Audre, 113
Lyotard, J.F., 19

MacAulay, Donna, 58
McDermott, Kathleen, 38
McRobbie, Angela, 98
Maguire, Patricia, 16, 32
Ma Mawi Wi Chi Itata, 24
Manitoba Association of Women's Shelters (MAWS), 61
Martindale, Kathleen, 81
Meaning, construction of, 6, 95
Medicine Wheel, 25–6, 31, 32
Methods, research: as 'culture', 9; 'feminist', 49; multiple, ix, 12, 14, 48, 51 (*see also* Triangulation); qualitative/quantitative, 49; *see also* Creative analyses; Document analysis; Interviews; Questionnaires
Milliken, Eveline, 33
Mount Cashel Orphanage, 107, 110–11

Narratives: 'grand' (meta-), 4, 6, 19, 59; 'micro-', 5
National Coalition Against Domestic Violence (NCADV; US), 93
National Welfare Grants (NWG), 103–4, 105, 106, 111, 112
'Natural laws', 4
Needs assessments, 59–62; sample questions, 125–7
Neuman, Mallory, 33

Objectivity, 4, 70, 105–6, 113

Ontology, 115
Organizational structure: collective, 35, 54, 55, 56; 'feminist', 45-6
Organizations, alternative, 35, 45-6 (*see also* Collectives); and power, 55

Paglia, Camille, 100
'Paralysis', 16, 49
Pearson, Gerry, 64
Performance, social, 77, 115
Perrault, Sharon, 24–31
Phelan, Shane, 8
Phenomenology, 116
Positivism, 4, 5, 70, 73, 116
Postmodernism, ix, x, 4, 32–3, 116; and feminism, 97–8; feminist, 4, 5, 115; and identity, 13; and 'interruption', x, 1, 4, 5, 6–7 (*see also* Links); *see also* Deconstruction
Poststructuralism, 5
Power, 116; balancing, 25, 32; critical analysis of, 9–12; and feminism, 68–9; and knowledge, 67, 71, 77; and language, 6, 9–10, 100 (*see also* Discourse); 'microphysics of', 65, 66; in organizations, 40, 42, 44–5, 46; 'power plays', 66, 69–71, 79, 116; and race, 28, 32; as relational, 4, 10; in research relationships, 2, 3, 9–10, 15, 63, 65–91, 97; responsible use of, 2, 9, 10, 80
Praxis, 5, 116

Question, research, 17, 20, 21, 24–5, 128
Questionnaires, 53, 55, 56, 60, 61; sample, 117–22

Racism, 23, 32, 55
Rappaport, Julian, 2
Reflexivity, 5, 13, 17, 35, 48, 56, 57, 58, 66, 68, 79, 98, 128, 130; and flexibility, 48; and research design, 48, 49; and research methods, 48; and 'paralysis', 49; as reality check, 50
Renzetti, Claire, 72
Research: and advocacy, 51, 105–6; collaborative/participatory, 11, 12, 16, 17, 25, 49, 61, 78, 82-3, 92, 95, 99, 102-3, 105, 112, 113, 115; 'grounding', 103–6; integrity, 50, 68, 69, 72, 77; limitations, 68; and marginalized groups, 2, 68, 73, 74, 105 (*see also* Lesbian research); positivist, 79;